ME, A PIECE OF WOOD, AND SIX STRINGS

HOW GUITAR AND MUSIC CHANGED A MAN'S LIFE

DAN FLOCKHART

For Mom

ME, A PIECE OF WOOD, AND SIX STRINGS

ISBN 978-0-9773585-8-8

Cover Design by Hannah Linder Designs

hannahlinderdesigns.com

CONTENTS

INTRODUCTION

"It's all happening"[1] Penny Lane

This is a book for music lovers. It's a story about guitar and music and how they make me feel like a little boy again. It's also a testimonial to my lifelong love affair with music. As such, it can be enjoyed equally by those who play guitar and those who don't.

Most people enjoy music, but why? Why do we like certain songs? Why do we love choruses so much? How does music impact the brain? How many people do not like music? Why is music so strongly associated with memories? Why does music have such an impact on our lives? What is the best metric to judge the popularity of songs? What are the greatest songs of all time? What are the most recognizable songs and earworms? What are the greatest soundtracks from films? This book looks at these topics and more, including how I maximize my potential, music's role in my planned wedding proposal at the top of a lighthouse in the ocean, and my lifetime list of 700 favorite songs covering 53 years, beginning when I was 11 years old.

There's something in it for everyone, and there are plenty of juicy tidbits along the way.

During the last year, I read a dozen autobiographies written by legendary musicians. They were filled with inspiration, humor, and compelling stories. But I was looking for more. I wanted to know how long it took them to be able to play chords, how long before they could play in tempo, how long before they could play their first song? What was their first song, what were their struggles, and how many hours a day did they practice? What were their first guitars, who were their biggest influences, and who were their most important teachers? What was their learning process and how long did it take to become a competent guitar player? Do they still play and if so, how many hours a day? Have their skills deteriorated over the last 40 years? What are their favorite chords, songs, artists, and albums? These questions acted as a catalyst for part of this book. Actually, this tome is really two books in one. Some chapters focus on guitar while other chapters cover a wide range of topics in music. Other than Chapter Nine, there are only a couple of paragraphs that might be a little technical for people who don't play guitar.

Hopefully, one day a vaccine will end the COVID-19 nightmare, but until then, how do we get through it? Since infectious disease experts believe staying indoors could be the new normal, how do we bide our time while staying indoors?

One answer is music. Case in point: I'm a 63-year-old disabled guitar player who began playing at age 58. I'm missing a finger on my left hand, had an operation on my right arm that reduced my range of motion, and I have small hands that lack flexibility. In other words, the odds are stacked against me. However, I'm having the time of my life. In fact, as I write this, I haven't left my house for almost three months, in large part because I am content with my guitar and I don't get bored. After all, there has never been a better time to learn how to play guitar (or any instrument, for that matter) than right now. Indeed, imagine how prolific musicians are in the current pandemic climate, hunkered down indoors writing songs and creating music. I would not be surprised to see an avalanche of incredible music released in the next few years.

So why did I write this book? Was it to learn about myself, express my creativity, or reflect on a lifetime of listening to music? Or maybe I wanted to describe my passion, inspire people to play guitar, or document the challenges I faced? Perhaps my goal was to entertain readers (or myself), or share my love of music with the world?

The answer is all of the above. Writing this book gave me the opportunity to reflect on my life, and with it, some long-forgotten memories. In the end, that's all we really have, memories.

We all have a story to tell. Hopefully, this book can inspire you to tell your story. I hope you enjoy it.

CHAPTER ONE

SECRET WEAPON

Music . . . speaks in emotions, and if it's in the bones, it's in the bones."[1] Keith Richards

I HAVE a secret weapon in my house. She's always waiting for me to pick her up so she can help me get in touch with my inner rock star. Indeed, she has the extraordinary power to make me feel like I'm Springsteen. And that, my friends, is priceless.

Guitar has to be one of the greatest hobbies in the history of mankind. It provides a pathway to my higher consciousness, allows me to dream while I'm awake, and takes me to the edge of the universe where another dimension exists. It launches me into a time-warp vortex where I can touch the stars, find life in black holes, and live for eternity. It's like taking a tequila shot of energy from the center of the sun and then hitching a ride on a rocket ship to another galaxy. Plus, it's free and I can do it every day.

Music is the special sauce in life, and guitars are the magic ingredient. With one strum, it's in my bones. It's a miracle.

Suddenly, I've recaptured my youth. I feel like a boy again. My brain fires on all cylinders. My heart explodes with joy. All resentments are forgiven. I'm lost in another world. Time ceases to exist. There is no past or future, only now. It's just me, a piece of wood, and six strings.

Learning how to play guitar has changed my life. It inspires me, feeds my creativity, and makes me feel alive. I get goosebumps at least once a day while I play. I feel like I'm the luckiest guy on the planet. I cannot imagine living without my "girl." I wonder how many other senior citizens wake up every day excited to get at their hobby first thing in the morning.

The single greatest thing about guitar is the feeling it gives me when I play. Many have tried to explain this feeling but have failed, because words cannot adequately convey feelings. It's unlike anything I've felt before, a mind-body connection that is orgasmic, deep, and profound. It's a phenomenon, really. When I play, I am struck with wonder and awe at the indescribable feeling permeating throughout my body. The world would be a better place if everyone could experience this feeling, because there is something about playing guitar that brings out the best in human potential, a step closer to self-actualization.

Playing guitar can make me feel powerful, happy, compassionate, vulnerable, or emotional. Sometimes these feelings can occur almost simultaneously. The sound emanating from a guitar can be joyful, haunting, soothing, intense, or melancholy. Consequently, guitar is a powerful medium to express feelings that perhaps cannot be articulated, an auditory manifestation of emotions, if you will. This is one of the reasons guitars are popular, because they help us to express how we really feel.

A few years ago my wife and I lost both of our dogs (an English bulldog and a Corgi). They were the heart and soul of our family, and I went through a brutal grieving process. During that time, I fell in love with my guitar. It provided comfort and gave me hope. The tears flowed when I played and it helped to heal my broken heart. Likewise, I recently had an accident in my backyard that left deep cuts on my legs. A few days later I got bit by a tick, and as I write this I'm waiting for test results to see if the tick carries the bacteria responsible for Lyme disease. I am worried and have been unable to think of little else, except when I play. It helps to put my mind at ease.

Like many individuals, I get lonely. Actually, loneliness has been one of my most prevalent feelings during my life. I've never felt like I fit in anywhere. I have a recurring dream that I'm late for school (i.e., my subconscious telling me I'm not prepared to learn whatever lesson the universe may have in store for me), and when I finally arrive, I feel like I don't fit in. Even prior to the pandemic, I had almost no social life. So what do I do when I'm lonely? I'll give you one guess.

Nothing brings me greater joy than playing guitar, with the exception of hugging my wife or playing with my pets. When things are not going well in my life, all I have to do is pick up my girl, and my faith in humanity is restored. Two hours has never gone by so quickly. I can unleash my stress and express myself through my own songs. It's the best therapy in the world. Indeed, I feel lost if a day goes by and I don't play.

During these perilous times when fear is pervasive and anxiety reigns, guitar keeps me grounded. My worries melt away when I play. Nothing else feels so right or so meaningful. I am never more certain of my purpose in life than when I play. It's a direct link to fulfillment and spiritual awakening, the nexus of cosmic energy and divine intervention.

One of the coolest things about guitar is I can play some of my all-time favorite songs. All it takes is time and anybody can do it. It has nothing to do with talent, it's simply muscle memory. All it takes is practice, practice, and more practice. The only cost is time and the reward is more than I could've imagined. And I found plenty of people who helped guide me along the way.

According to Willie Nelson, "The wisdom is in the moments when the madness slips away and we remember the basics."[2] I can't think of a better way to "let go of the madness and remember the basics" than playing guitar. It's organic, primal, and soothes my soul. I don't need a cell phone or the latest gadget or the Internet. All I need is a guitar and I'm on the road to a higher plane.

In the midst of the coronavirus pandemic, I think of my guitar as my "vaccine," because I'm content not leaving the house and therefore I'm safe. I can only imagine the time wasted by adolescents as they bury their faces in electronic gadgets all day long, and yet they could be learning a new hobby that could bring them immense joy. Given that families are quarantining together and we may have more viruses in the future, this pandemic is an opportunity to learn how to play guitar, perhaps facilitating family sing-alongs. Instead of boredom, they could blast off toward the heavens, kiss the cosmos, salute Xanadu, and continue on to Shangri-La. Serenity is only a guitar away.

All humans are tortured souls at some point in their lives. During those times, we look for comfort and familiarity. Guitar is a constant in my life I can always count on. My "baby" is always there. She does not criticize, she does not judge, she does not talk behind my back, and she's always waiting for me. I feel better and have a clearer perspective after I spend time with her. I am truly content and feel newfound hope after I play every day. Isn't that the point?

According to country music star Brad Paisley, "Some of my best friends are guitars."[3] I couldn't agree more. You might ask, "How can an inanimate object be a friend? Well, if the definition of a friend is someone or something that brings you joy, peace, comfort, and support, and is reliable, sensitive, and loyal, well then, welcome to how guitar players feel about their guitars. Certainly, some guitarists often choose to play guitar instead of spending time with friends (or family). Case in point: For my

60th birthday, my wife bought me tickets to a San Francisco 49ers football game. It was an opportunity to see my beloved team play against Tom Brady, considered one of the greatest quarterbacks of all time. The weather report called for a storm, and I didn't want to make a 12 hour round-trip in that weather when I could stay home, build a fire, and play guitar. Given that it was my birthday and I wanted to do what I wanted to do on that day, I decided to stay home.

One of the reasons I love playing guitar is because it allows me to live in the moment. I spent too much time thinking about the future when I was younger, and now that I'm older I spend too much time thinking about the past. Meanwhile, volumes have been written linking happiness and contentment with living in the moment. Playing guitar gives me the opportunity to just "be." It's not a coincidence that I am happiest when I play.

For some people who live on the streets, a guitar may be their only friend. One young man told me guitar saved his life when he was homeless. His guitar meant the world to him because it was the only way he could escape reality, even for a brief moment in time, a moment where he could experience the joy of music. This moment allowed him to become fully engaged in his imagination and surrender to the universe. It gave him the opportunity to live in the moment and not worry about where his next meal would come from.

When I pick up my guitar, I feel like somebody has given me an incredible gift, so I better not waste time. It's such a treat, better than Christmas morning. When I launch into my first song, I know with every bone in my body that out of all the things I could be doing, I am doing the one thing that I most want to do. It's the greatest feeling in the world. This is why so many guitar players consider themselves the luckiest people alive.

I used to play golf when I was a young man. Like all golfers,

I enjoyed the sensation when the ball struck the sweet spot on the clubface. It was a great feeling, especially when I saw the ball fly off into the distance toward the target. I used to shoot in the mid-80s on a par 72 course, which meant that I had roughly 36 chances from the tees and fairways to hit the sweet spot in 4 1/2 hours, the time spent for a usual round of golf. I never counted the number of times I hit the sweet spot, but it wasn't 36. Compare this scenario to playing guitar and hitting the sweet spot with every strum. The feeling of hitting the sweet spot in golf pales in comparison to how I feel when I'm strumming and dialed in on my acoustic. When I play for a couple of hours, I hit thousands of sweet spots (I did the math). Heck, I hit 36 sweet spots in the first 15 seconds when I begin playing every day. It's an amazing feeling. It sports, it's called being "in the zone." Imagine having something in your house you can pick up and immediately get into the zone. This is why guitars are such good friends. They make you feel good. Actually, I told my wife that if I'm not home and our house catches on fire, the first thing she needs to grab is my guitar.

There are several reasons why guitar is one of world's most popular instruments. They are portable, polyphonic, and seductive. They can help improve memory, communication, and motor skills. Playing guitar can lower blood pressure, release dopamine in the brain, and strengthen the tendons and muscles in the arms, wrists, and hands. Guitar can reduce stress, boost confidence, and provide a mechanism for the healing process. It can also improve focus, spread joy, and empower others. Moreover, there's nothing like the sound of an acoustic guitar with the human voice.

There is another advantage to playing guitar. The state where I live has frequent power shortages. If the power goes out, all I have to do is pick up my acoustic. It's great to practice in the dark because I can't see the fretboard and therefore have to rely on pure feel.

Guitars also have a low carbon footprint, require little maintenance, and are inexpensive to maintain. Once you buy a guitar, the only additional cost is strings, which is nominal. The cost for a starter guitar is relatively low as well. There are decent entry-level acoustics for the price of a nice dinner and a bottle of wine.

CHAPTER TWO

FIFTY YEARS

"Music gives a soul to the universe, wings to the mind, flight to the imagination and life to everything."[1] Plato

SO HOW DOES music change my life? That's easy. I look at my life as a series of feelings and experiences from one moment to the next. My life is the sum of those feelings and experiences. Music can instantaneously change how I feel, which in turn impacts my experience at any given time.

I was raised in a family that didn't express emotions. Consequently, I didn't know how to deal with my feelings for the first 30 years of my life. Then my dad died. Music helped me to feel, to get in touch with feelings I didn't want to feel. It was cathartic.

Music has been the love of my life for 50 years. It takes me to heights I didn't know I could feel. It has a remarkable power and I draw from it every day. However, I didn't realize how important it was to me until I taught at a private school in the San Francisco Bay Area during the 1990s. Each year, I took the seventh-grade students on a weeklong field study trip to

Yosemite National Park. One day we were sitting on the trail when the field guide asked the students, "What could you not live without?" One student said she could not live without music. Her answer resonated with me because I felt the same way, and I realized consciously for the first time how important music was in my life.

As a former teacher, I used to drive into the school parking each day cranking Better Than Ezra or Third Eye Blind. I didn't drink coffee, so that was how I woke myself up. Minutes later, I was in chapel singing hymns with the students. I was struck by the dissonance between cranking rock tunes and singing hymns, within minutes of each other.

Music has never been as ubiquitous as it is today. It doesn't matter where you live, you cannot escape it. From mountain climbers listening to their iPods to astronauts listening in space, you could be hundreds of miles from civilization and run into someone singing your song. This happened to Roger Daltrey (The Who), who met two guys on a hike in the middle of nowhere who were singing one of his songs.[2] Truly, music is a global force and brings the world closer.

Virtually every culture has engaged in musical endeavors, some of which date back 250,000 years.[3] Which begs the question, what would the world be like if music didn't exist? For starters, I would not have met my wife because we met at a ballroom dancing event. Without music, dancing wouldn't exist. In effect, my love of music led me to an event where I met my wife. It was serendipity at first dance.

Additionally, if music did not exist, there would be no "Happy Birthday," song, no "Star-Spangled Banner," no "God Bless America," no "Take Me Out to the Ballgame," no opera, no Broadway, no music in films or television, no portable music players, no cruising to tunes on Saturday night, no singing in church, no music industry, no concerts, no rock 'n roll, no jazz, no soul, no country, no hip hop, and no music from the likes of

Bruce Springsteen, Elvis Presley, Chuck Berry, Bob Marley, James Brown, Marvin Gaye, Miles Davis, John Coltrane, the Beatles, Pink Floyd, or Led Zeppelin. The list goes on and on. Imagine the shower scene in *Psycho* without music, or *Jaws* without its pulsating soundtrack, or *Star Wars* without its theme song. Fred Astaire would not have danced in the rain. What would Springsteen or Jimmy Page be doing these days without music? What about Keith Richards and Mick Jagger? Paul McCartney? It boggles the mind to consider a world without music.

My life, like many people, has been defined by music. Songs evoke memories from our childhood that take us back to a specific place and time. Consequently, music is a powerful marker in our lives. For instance, I'll never forget when I was at a friend's house 50 years ago listening to "Suite Judy Blue Eyes" for the first time, and falling in love with their catchy harmonies, especially at the end of the song. The song builds up to the outro and it's simply unforgettable, similar to the chorus in the Beatles' "Hey Jude." Likewise, I'll never forget a romantic interlude with a woman in college while James Taylor played in the background on my stereo. You've got a friend, indeed.

We had something called "Flex Day" when I was in high school. Students could sign up to go to any classes they wanted. It was so poorly managed by the administration that students "flexed" into the local burger joint or skipped school altogether. Then they forged teacher signatures to prove they were in class. I flexed into a music class, which meant I could listen to music on headphones for 45 minutes. And I could do that twice a day. For this reason, I thought Flex Day was the greatest invention ever. I still remember listening to The Doobie Brothers' "Jesus is Just Alright" during those sessions. I never heard anything like that before. A year later they released *The Captain and Me* album, which I listened to throughout the remainder of my high school years.

I have memories of many songs when I was young, even if the memory was simply listening to the song in my bedroom. The list is extensive, but in particular, songs like America's "A Horse with No Name," Jim Croce's "Time in a Bottle," Tommie Roe's "Dizzy," Glen Campbell's "Galveston," Blood, Sweat & Tears' "Spinning Wheel," The Zombies' "Time of the Season," and the O'Jays' "Back Stabbers" bring back strong memories. The same goes for "So Very Hard to Go" by Tower of Power, one of my Top 10 songs of all time. Additionally, anytime I hear a song by one of the "hair bands" of the 1980s (Poison, Def Leppard, Cinderella, White Snake, RATT, Warrant, Quiet Riot, Bon Jovi, Motley Crue, Twisted Sister), I have fond memories of watching MTV videos with friends during the early 1980s.

Every time I hear a song by The Babys, it takes me back to a beautiful valley about an hour from my hometown. Why? Once, on my way to college, I reached the crest of the valley as I listened to the climax of "Dying Man." It was a serendipitous moment that has stuck with me for 40 years. (By the way, I believe The Babys are one of the most underrated groups of all time). Perhaps the reason I still remember this is the fact that my college roommate had recently installed a device in my 1972 Ford Pinto that allowed me to listen to headphones. I thought I was in heaven, although I wonder how I can still hear anything given the amount of time I spent listening to loud music in my headphones, as well as all the concerts I went to.

I'll also never forget playing badminton in college on a volleyball court while listening to REO Speedwagon's "Ridin' the Storm Out." We played for hours and listened to dozens of songs but for some reason that's the one song that stands out to me now.

When I hear Neil Young's "Heart of Gold," I think of the portable radio my family had in our sunroom that we listened to before we went to school each day. The radio station played too many commercials so I called them. When the DJ answered, I said, "Play some music," and then hung up. It was not my finest hour. This was before I had a stereo and I wanted to hear some good tunes in the morning before I went to school. It was an AM radio station, the only one in the rural town where I was raised. This is why I was excited whenever I traveled to the San Francisco Bay Area, because it gave me a chance to listen to FM radio. I couldn't believe they played all music, all the time. I thought it was nirvana for music lovers. Forty years later, the same concept applies to satellite radio; I had a long commute to work before I retired but I didn't mind so much because I got lost in the music.

Every time I hear The Knack's "My Sharona," I think of a donut shop in my college town. I have no idea why; I guess the song was playing there one night when we had the munchies. I loved the solo in that song, and the album was played at numerous parties. It topped the charts at Number One in the US in 1979. A year later, their second album peaked at Number 15, and a year after that their third album peaked at Number 93.[4] Perhaps what they say is true, that you're only as good as your last record. However, when album sales decrease significantly, does that mean the quality of the music is lower, or the public had certain expectations based on the prior album and therefore those expectations were not met? I've heard plenty of albums that were better than their predecessor even though the number of albums sold decreased significantly. In the case of The Knack, I guess people were expecting more "My Sharonas," but it didn't turn out that way.

Rod Stewart's "Maggie May" brings back memories of playing it on the jukebox at the local bowling alley when I was a kid. Likewise, when I hear Kenny Chesney's "California," it takes me back to when my girlfriend (now my wife of 20+ years) and I saw him play at the county fair in Merced, California. I was in love with her and I dreamed that it might be our wedding song. However, we didn't have a wedding song because we eloped to Las Vegas. The irony here is the only aspect of getting married that I ever thought about was the wedding song, but we don't have one. C'est la vie.

The quantity, quality, and diversity of the music released when I was in high school and college (the 1970s) was extraordinary. The list of artists who released debut albums during that decade was stunning, and many of those debut albums are now considered classics. I go back to those days every time I hear a song from The Car's debut album, and what an album it was. "Just What I Needed," "My Best Friend's Girl," "You're All I've Got Tonight," and "Bye-Bye Love" are classics. Also, my generation will never forget Boston's debut LP. It was a game changer. However, my favorite debut album during that time was by The Pretenders. I played it every day when it came out. Chrissie Hynde looked like the baddest woman in the universe on the cover.

Consider the influence and scope of the artists below (a random list) who released their debut albums during the 1970s:

1971

- America
- Bonnie Raitt
- Carly Simon
- ZZ Top
- The Doobie Brothers
- Crazy Horse
- Earth Wind and Fire
- Electric Light Orchestra

1972

- Blue Oyster Cult
- Roxy Music
- Steely Dan

- Michael Jackson
- Jackson Browne
- Bette Midler
- Eagles
- Lou Reed
- Styx
- Peter Frampton

1973

- Aerosmith
- Bachman-Turner Overdrive
- Barry Manilow
- Bruce Springsteen
- Queen
- Montrose
- New York Dolls
- Lynyrd Skynyrd
- Abba
- Barry White

1974

- Bad Company
- KISS
- Rush
- Todd Rundgren

1975

- Journey
- Patti Smith
- Ted Nugent
- AC/DC

- Dr. Feelgood
- Outlaws
- Heart

1976

- Blondie
- Boston
- The Ramones
- The Runaways
- Tom Petty and the Heartbreakers

1977

- Bjork
- Peter Gabriel
- Cheap Trick
- The Clash
- Talking Heads
- Elvis Costello
- Sex Pistols

1978

- The Cars
- Buzzcocks
- Prince
- Van Halen
- Kate Bush
- The Police
- Devo
- Dire Straits

1979

- B-52s
- Pat Benatar
- The Knack
- The Cure
- Joe Jackson
- The Human League
- Simple Minds

Not only does music take us back to a certain place and time in our lives, it reminds us of people. For instance, I think of an old friend when I hear any song from Elton John's *Goodbye Yellow Brick Road*. I also think of friends when I hear any song by the Eagles, Billy Joel, Jackson Browne, Earth, Wind, and Fire, Blue Oyster Cult, Hush, Robin Trower, Jimi Hendrix, and Pablo Cruise, among others. Remember "Hold On Loosely," by 38 Special? For some reason, and I don't know why, when I hear that song I think about a double play I turned in a men's softball league when I was in my mid-20s. I was playing second base and the ball was hit to the shortstop; as I came across the bag to get the throw I barehanded it and in one motion fired to first base for the double play. I guess that was my 38 Special.

They say music is a universal language. They also say the same thing about mathematics, but it's difficult to imagine any aspect of life that connects so many people and touches so many lives like music. Indeed, can you think of a time when you formed a connection with someone through music? It happened to me when I was a young man on a date in San Francisco. I asked her to name her favorite albums. She couldn't remember the name of one of the bands but she remembered the album cover. I asked her to give me a hint about the cover. She said "trees." I immediately said Pablo Cruise. Of all the albums ever released, I guessed the correct one, although it didn't hurt that I actually had that album. Needless to say, my date was impressed and we had already formed a connection through music.

Simply hearing someone's name can act as a catalyst to music. For example, when I meet someone named Roxanne, the first thing I think about is the song by The Police as well as Eddie Murphy singing it in his jail cell at the beginning of the film *48 Hours*. If I meet someone named Jessie, I immediately think of "Jessie's Girl" by Rick Springfield. The same holds true if I meet someone named Daniel (Elton John), Fernando (Abba), Mandy (Barry Manilow), or Michelle (Beatles).

This brings up an interesting question, what is the most famous song title that includes a name?

- Billie Jean
- Help Me, Rhonda
- Jumpin' Jack Flash
- Lucy in the Sky with Diamonds
- Gloria
- Layla
- Louie Louie
- Hey Jude
- Johnny B. Goode
- Eleanor Rigby
- Rhiannon
- Mack the Knife
- Me and Bobby McGee
- Lola
- Roxanne
- Maggie May
- Sweet Jane
- Sweet Baby James
- The Ghost of Tom Joad
- Rosalita

- Cecilia
- Lovely Rita
- Brandy
- Mustang Sally
- Good Golly Miss Molly
- Sweet Caroline
- The Wind Cries Mary
- Bette Davis Eyes

THERE ARE several characteristics of music that I'm grateful for. For instance, I enjoy the way songs grow on me. If I like a song the first time I hear it, then I know I'm going to eventually love it. We've all had the experience when we're not sure if we like a song after the first listen, but the more we listen, the more we like it because we become familiar with it. After all, familiarity breeds comfort.

If I heard a song I liked on the radio when I was a kid, I was forced to buy the entire album, provided the artist did not release the song as a single. When I purchased an album, there were four potential outcomes: I was disappointed because I didn't like any songs other than the song I purchased the album for, or I thought some of the other songs were okay so I was fairly neutral about laying out the cash for the purchase, or I was pleasantly surprised because I liked most of the songs, or I was out of my mind because I thought the album was fantastic. However, there was a caveat in that if the one song I purchased the album for was truly incredible, then the disappointment from the rest of the album was mitigated somewhat.

I usually don't like every song on an album. In fact, there are only a handful of albums where I like every song. I usually like individual songs, and specifically, parts of songs. I'll play songs over and over just to get to the good part, maybe the chorus or a guitar solo or a great drumbeat. For instance, take the outro (beginning at 3:53) of Third Eye Blind's "The Red Summer Sun." It's beautiful and haunting, and the drummer absolutely kills it. I can't help but listen to it several times in a row. And I'm not the only person who loves it. Pull it up on YouTube and read the comments.

Additional songs where I find myself waiting in anticipation include "Neil's Fandango" and "Without You" by The Doobie Brothers. I look forward to the solos in those songs. I get the same feeling when Tommy Bolin begins his solo in Deep Purple's "Gettin' Tighter," or when Jimi Hendrix starts his solo in "All Along the Watchtower," or when Alvin Lee begins his solo in "I'd Love to Change the World." The list goes on and on.

As a teenager, few things in life were more thrilling than buying a record from an artist I never heard of, only to discover it was a great album. This has been one of my favorite things in life - the continual quest for new music - not only new music but the kind of music that brings me home when I'm on the road. There's a line from the film *Almost Famous*, when William Miller tells Penny Lane that he has to go home. Lane replies, "You are home."[5] That's how I feel about music. It's always there, never lets me down, and can help take the pain away in trying times. And it's free on YouTube.

When I was young, I was fired up when I got my hands on a new record. The excitement built the closer I got to home, as I rode my bike at supersonic speeds while jumping curbs and gutters. It was an indescribable feeling. The process is different in today's climate because music is streamed online, so there is no need to rush home from the record store. However, I still have to wait until new music is released so anticipation still builds. Actually, as I write this, Springsteen is set to release his first rock 'n roll album in years sometime this year. I'm looking forward to it.

When I buy new music, I'll often play it over and over again to the point where I can get tired of it within a day or two. I then need to take some time off from the song because there is something about listening to a song with fresh ears. Or perhaps I didn't like a song in the first place. For example, songs I don't like include "Gloria," "Kung Fu Fighting," and "Rock the Boat." There's nothing wrong with the songs; I simply don't care for them. And I'm in the minority, because they were hit songs. There are countless songs that reach the top of the charts that I don't care for. My favorite songs are often those that get the least amount of response, at least according to iTunes. Maybe it's my age and the fact that most people on iTunes are from the younger generation, therefore our musical tastes are different?

Even though I'm a music lover, I know people who listen to music more than I do and have much larger record collections. But does that mean they love music more than I do? To find out, we would need to quantify the pleasure we feel when we listen to music. Perhaps neurologists can already do this by attaching electrodes to the cortex and monitoring pleasure levels in the brain as we listen? If so, this could lead to some interesting data. For instance, given that dopamine levels in adults can decrease by up to 10% every decade, it is likely that teenagers would have higher scores than Paul McCartney because their dopamine levels could be approximately 50% higher than McCartney, who is approaching 80 years old.[6] This brings up a host of questions. Who would have the highest score in the world? Could scores be correlated to the genre people prefer? Would musicians have higher scores than non-musicians? Which occupations would have the highest scores? Which countries would have overall higher marks than others? Would there be a difference in scores between genders? Would there be differences in scores based on income levels, given that lower income is associated with a lower-quality diet, primarily due to lack of fruits and vegetables, the very foods that increase dopamine levels?

(Diet and lifestyle factors influence dopamine levels, which I discuss in Chapter 11).

Let's assume that dopamine levels decrease by 10% every decade. Therefore, if I had 100% of my dopamine levels at age 20, then I had 90% at age 30, 80% at age 40, 70% at age 50, and 60% at age 60. Since I'm approaching 64, this means it's possible my dopamine levels are trending down to almost half of what I was born with. Perhaps this explains why I don't laugh nearly as much as I used to or why I don't feel the same intensity of pleasure like I did when I was young. This might also explain my quest for new music; I'm trying to match the pleasure I felt when I listened to music as a teenager. However, guitar is somewhat of an equalizer because my dopamine kicks into gear when I play.

Perhaps decreasing dopamine levels over time helps to explain why so many music lovers from older generations believe the music they grew up with was better than the music put out today. They had significantly more dopamine levels so they enjoyed music more. Here's an exercise for you: Pull up some music from the 60s or 70s on YouTube. Then read the comments below the video. Chances are several of the comments lament the current state of music and believe they grew up with the best music, no matter the decade. Is this because the grass is always greener when it comes to nostalgia? Or is it decreasing dopamine levels? Or both?

While on the topic of dopamine, if it was possible to measure the aggregate pleasure level of the audience at a concert, would the average pleasure level per fan be lower today than it was in the pre-cell phone era? Recently, I watched videos of concerts from the 80s, before cell phones existed. It seemed like the fans were living more in the moment with the music, versus the current generation where many fans try to capture video on their cell phones rather than enjoy the moment for what it is. It makes me wonder, why do so many people try to capture video at concerts? Do they watch it later? Do they want to hold onto it for posterity? Is it mainly to show off to their friends? Do they want to post it to their social media accounts to give people the impression they are happier than they really are?

THERE HAVE BEEN volumes written about the power of music to inspire. But what does music inspire us to do? It could include moving forward in life, forgiving friends, getting sober, creating art, facing fears, applying for a dream job, going back to school, or initiating a difficult conversation with a friend. One way music inspires me is through the ideas that come to me when I listen. My best ideas seem to occur when I'm listening to music. There is something about the medium that opens me up to all possibilities in the universe.

As we mature, our musical tastes evolve. For instance, a recent newspaper article listed relevant song titles for the COVID-19 pandemic. Some readers mentioned Mozart, Bach, or other classical composers. Would those readers have selected those artists when they were in high school? Perhaps some, but certainly not many. Their musical tastes have evolved. Meanwhile, I listed songs by Tom Petty, Creedence Clearwater Revival, and Crosby, Stills and Nash, among others. I wondered whether most people my age listen to rock 'n roll anymore. I'd like to know the percentage of people in their 60s who regularly listen to rock 'n roll compared to the percentage of people in their 20s. I certainly don't listen to rock 'n roll nearly as much as I did when I was a young man. My musical tastes have mellowed. Perhaps the question is moot since rock 'n roll seems to be a dying breed among the younger generation.

At any rate, here's my list of relevant song titles while living in the midst of a pandemic:

- It's the End of the World as We Know It by REM
- Carry On by CSN&Y
- Even in the Quietest Moments by Supertramp
- What is and What Should Never Be by Led Zeppelin
- I'd Love to Change the World by Ten Years After
- Don't Worry Be Happy by Bobby McFerrin
- I Want to Hold Your Hand by the Beatles
- Help! by the Beatles
- Under Pressure by David Bowie
- Bad Moon Rising by Creedence Clearwater Revival
- Day After Day by Badfinger
- Jesus, Take the Wheel by Carrie Underwood
- American Pie by Don McLean
- World in Changes by Dave Mason
- Let it Be by the Beatles
- Don't Come Around Here No More by Tom Petty and the Heartbreakers
- Knockin' on Heaven's Door by Bob Dylan
- It's Too Late by Carol King
- Ain't No Mountain High Enough by The Supremes
- The Times They Are a-Changin' by Bob Dylan
- Stayin' Alive by the Bee Gees
- Don't Stand so Close to Me by the Police
- With a Little Help From My Friends by the Beatles
- Feel Like Makin' Love by Bad Company

TRUE MUSIC LOVERS do not care about genres. For example, I know a young guitarist in his 20s who plays rock 'n roll. Music is his life. When I asked him to name some of the artists he enjoyed listening to, the first name he gave me was Taylor Swift. I was surprised at his answer but it goes to show that if people like a song, they like a song, no matter the genre. Personally, I don't care who the artist is or what genre it fits into. If a song elicits emotion or connects with me on some level, that's all I need. If I like it, I like it.

Contrast this scenario with people who don't like country, rock, soul, jazz, or other genres. By purposely not listening to specific genres, they might be missing out on some great songs because many songs incorporate multiple genres and have strong crossover appeal. How many times have you been surprised by a song from an artist that you normally wouldn't listen to? In music, as in life, it pays to be open-minded.

And just how many genres are there? It depends on the source. There are hundreds listed on Wikipedia. Or consider data-alchemist Glenn McDonald's list of 1,264 micro-genres found on his website Every Noise at Once.[7] It's an algorithmically-generated scatterplot based on data tracked and analyzed by Spotify. Simply click on a genre to listen to an example and see a list of artists in a scatterplot format from that genre. It's an amazing map.

Which begs the question, "Are we what we listen to?" And if so, what if we listen to everything, all genres? Does this mean we are more musically evolved than someone who only listens to one genre? Take people who believe classical music is superior to other genres and thus believe they have superior musical tastes. But what if they only listen to that one genre? Even through that genre may have more complex arrangements, does that make them more musically evolved than someone who listens to hip-hop, country, rock, pop, *and* electronic? In other words, does the diversity of our playlists reflect how musically evolved we are? Perhaps a more thought-provoking question would be, "Out of all of the constructs in life, where does music rank in terms of its influence on human potential?"

I don't know the answer to those questions, but I do know the older I get, the more I enjoy listening to genres that I did not consider when I was a young man. For instance, here's an example of one of my current playlists:

- Miles Davis
- Luke Bryan
- Slushii
- Donny Hathaway
- Ten Years After
- II Divo
- Ne-Yo
- Kate Bush
- Neon Trees
- Van
- Everything But The Girl
- Jesse Cook
- The Spinners
- Led Zeppelin
- Roxette
- Cat Stevens
- April Wine
- Haux
- Journey
- Eric Church
- Luther Vandross
- Glen Campbell
- P.M. Dawn
- Joni Mitchell
- John Coltrane
- Old Dominion
- Supertramp
- St. Lucia
- Coldplay
- Neil Young
- Third Eye Blind

- Bruce Springsteen
- Halsey
- Rihanna
- Marvin Gaye
- Giraffage
- Keith Urban
- Thompson Square
- The Moody Blues
- Petit Biscuit
- Alicia Keys
- Bob Seger
- Porcupine Tree
- The Cure
- The Naked and Famous
- Better Than Ezra
- DJ Jazzy Jeff and the Fresh Prince
- The Phantom of the Opera soundtrack

CHAPTER THREE

I'LL TAKE IT

"Music is the universal language of mankind."[1]
Henry Wadsworth Longfellow

WHEN DO you feel most alive?

Perhaps many people would say during sex, but there are countless other intense moments. For instance, I feel alive whenever I cry. You can't feel the joy if you can't feel the pain, I always say.

I feel most alive when I'm creative. It feeds my soul and I could not live without it. The two most creative endeavors in my life have been writing books and playing guitar. Both of them feed my imagination and help me reflect on my life.

In 2015 I saw *Begin Again*, a film starring Adam Levine and Keira Knightley. Toward the end of the film, Levine performed an acoustic song called "Lost Stars." The song gave me goosebumps and I wanted to be able to play it. It was the first time I considered learning how to play guitar.

A few days later I walked into a music store with no idea of what I was going to buy. The owner suggested a $300 Recording

King guitar. He told me it was a good starter guitar and would do me well until I was ready to trade up at some point. He showed me how to form a G chord, but I couldn't stretch my fingers enough to get my pinky on the bottom string. Right then I knew I was in for a challenge, but that has never stopped me. Meanwhile, I heard someone in the back of the store playing "Babe I'm Gonna Leave You" by Led Zeppelin, which is my all-time favorite rock song. He was a high school student who had been playing for two years. (A high school kid playing Zeppelin? There is still hope in the world, I thought). I was excited because if he could do it, maybe I could as well? I brought the guitar home and my wife thought I was crazy.

I thought $300 would get me a decent starter guitar. I didn't want to pay more, just in case I couldn't play at all. I was skeptical in this regard because I completely ruptured my right bicep muscle five years earlier. When it happened, my bicep rolled up to my shoulder and freaked me out. I had surgery and was in a cast for seven weeks, which resulted in lost range of motion in my right wrist, which hinders my ability to play certain chords. I cannot fully supinate my right wrist, meaning if you touch your right elbow against the right side of your body and hold your arm so that your elbow bends at a 90° angle with your palm facing toward the left side of your body, then roll your wrist to the right, you will be able to roll your wrist so that the palm of your hand faces straight up. However, I can't do that.

Compounding my problem was the fact I lost my middle finger on my left hand in an industrial accident when I was in college. As a result, I'm forced to play left-handed because I want all of my fingers on my right hand available for the fretboard. A couple of instructors told me my dominant hand (my right hand) should be the strumming hand, but I followed my instinct and stayed with my right hand on the fretboard.

The only disadvantage to playing guitar left-handed is there is not a good supply of left-handed guitars in music stores.

However, two of the most famous and most accomplished guitarists of all time (Jimi Hendrix and Paul McCartney) are left-handed so I am in good company.

I believe one of the reasons many people quit guitar is because they try to form chords with their non-dominant hand. Several people have told me they tried to play guitar, but they were "not coordinated enough," or "it was too hard," or they told me, "I'm not musical." It's too bad because they are missing out on the opportunity of a lifetime of personal fulfillment and absolute joy. If they would spend 15 minutes a day for a couple of weeks, they would get to the point where they could transition between a few simple chords. Once they do that, they're on their way.

So, if you are reading this and you don't play guitar, are you willing to spend 15 minutes a day for two weeks in order to be able to begin playing songs? If you want to learn how to play an instrument, and your answer is no, ask yourself what is preventing you from experiencing the incredible joy of playing an instrument. Anybody can do it, there is no secret other than practice. So give it a shot. The effort is minimal compared to the reward.

But I digress. I'm right-handed so although it felt normal for me to have my right hand on the fretboard when I started, strumming was difficult with my non-dominant hand. The strumming hand is important because it controls the volume and tempo, and when I play fingerstyle or incorporate syncopation or arpeggiation, there can be a lot going on. But all it takes is practice.

On top of playing left-handed and having limited mobility, I had an operation on my eyes several years ago that left me farsighted. As a result, I wear bifocals when I play, one lens to see the strings and the second lens to see the lyrics on my music stand. However, even with glasses, the strings are a blur when I look down at them. In addition, my fingers are not as flexible as they once were, and I have small hands, a bad combination for a guitar player. In fact, every professional guitar player I've seen has large hands. Indeed, when it comes to guitar players, it's survival of the largest hands. Many famous licks are simple, but not always easy to replicate for someone with small hands. Flexibility can make up for small hands, but I have neither. However, I have the passion and work ethic, the most important traits when beginning any new endeavor.

Adolescents who have child-size hands at least have flexibility. So if you are reading this and you're on the younger side, please be aware that young people learn quicker, have flexibility in their fingers, and have the advantage of time. If you keep practicing, guitar will change your life, and you will then be able to inspire others to play.

The first day I started, I could not physically form any of the seven open chord shapes: A, B, C, D, E, F, and G. The only chord I could play clean was Em, which is considered one of the easier chords, but I couldn't even do that initially because I couldn't get my knuckles to bend enough and therefore my ring finger on the D string kept touching the G string (the next two paragraphs might be a little technical for readers who do not play guitar).

It took me two months to finally play a perfect G chord, and that was only after several seconds of trying to get it just right. I couldn't play a perfect G because my ring finger touched the A string underneath it. I couldn't bend my knuckles so that my ring and middle fingers were vertical enough. I moved my hand up around the neck so those two fingers were vertical but then my pinky couldn't reach the high E string. But even though I lightly touched (i.e., muted) the D string, it was still a G chord, although it didn't sound as big because I was missing the B note. But what was I going to do? The only people who can hear the difference are guitar players and it's not like I'm going to be on stage with the E Street Band anytime soon.

The same process applied to the C chord, where my ring

finger couldn't stretch to the end of the third fret on the A string. I had to consciously think about pressing it down hard to play it perfectly. Recently, I started playing C with my pinky on the A string while my ring finger rests on the low E string, since I'm strumming only the bottom five strings. There is more strength in the pinky than the ring finger and it's not nearly as much of a stretch.

The idea is to minimize movement on the fretboard. However, I'm constantly fighting the fretboard because of my immobility. It does not look pretty but with enough patience I can eventually play songs that I never thought I could play. Anytime I start feeling sorry for myself, I think of Django Reinhardt, a jazz guitarist from the early 1900s who played with only two fingers. There's even a person on YouTube who plays with his toes.[2] I cannot imagine that learning curve.

After a few weeks, I was able to successfully form three of the seven open chords (B and F were impossible and C and G were not perfect). I looked like a contortion artist as I struggled to position my body and arm to play B or F. I gave up on those chords for a couple of years before I started working on them again. To this day, I can't play B and F is not always clean. It is unbelievable how much time I've spent practicing this and I still don't have it, although it's getting closer. I hope so, it's only been five years! I simply refuse to believe that my physical limitations prevent me from playing these chords. If I'm getting closer, it tells me that eventually I can do it.

The first chord progression I was able to play while maintaining tempo was Fmaj7 to C. There's not much movement evolved, simply moving the second and third fingers up one string. I matched downstrokes to a slow four-count. Something inside my brain clicked and I thought, "So this is what it feels like." I suspect that everybody who plays guitar never forgets the first time they were able to put two chords together and keep time. What a feeling.

I signed up for lessons one month after I bought my guitar because I wanted to be able to play songs. During the first lesson, my instructor showed me a three-chord progression for Tom Petty's "Free Fallin." I practiced every day and I was able to play it after a couple of weeks. Guitar players might be surprised at how long it took me, but again, it's due to my limited mobility. I added extra strums when I hit the second verse. I also started to use dynamics, playing softer or louder to vary the sound. I was able to create my own version of the song. Then I experimented with a capo on the first three frets. They all sounded good but I discovered that my voice matched the song better with the capo in the first or second position.

I don't know if there's ever been another song so defined by the first two chords. Any rock 'n roll fan recognizes the song immediately after those chords. Petty was a brilliant songwriter and his lead guitarist (Mike Campbell) is an underrated guitar player. He can do it all. Petty and Campbell were a formidable combination, which is part of the reason The Heartbreakers' body of work stands up to any other American band.

I felt like a rock star when I was able to play this song. What an amazing feeling to be able to play one of the greatest songs of all time. This was also the first song I tried to sing and I was pleasantly surprised that I didn't sound that bad when I sang the chorus. I couldn't reach the high notes like Petty did, but it worked. It gave me immense joy and I wondered how Petty felt when he wrote this song. Did he know it was going to be a monster hit or did he think it was just another song?

By the way, I saw Tom Petty and The J. Geils Band in concert at the University of Davis in California when I was in college, circa 1978. I still remember thinking I was watching the two hottest bands in the world that night.

The next song I wanted to learn was Green Day's "Good Riddance," an iconic song played at countless graduation ceremonies. It's ironic that such a mellow song became Green Day's biggest hit, but that's the nature of the music business. I watched several covers on YouTube and most seemed to agree that the strumming pattern was DDU UDU, so that's what I went with. At this point I was introduced to a different G chord with the pinky and the ring finger on the high E and B strings. I needed to be able to do this because the chord that follows G is Cadd9, so I could leave my pinky and ring fingers on the first two strings as anchors. I only had to move my first and second fingers up one string so it was an easy switch. However, I couldn't play G perfectly because my middle finger on the low E string kept touching the A string. After I practiced for awhile, I found that it helped if I swung my elbow of my fretting arm away from my body. I still can't play it perfectly every time but it is what it is. The Cadd9 to G progression was a favorite of the "hair bands" in the 1980s because it sounded good and minimized movement on the fretboard. After Cadd9 to G, the song transitions to D, which I could do because I'd already learned it for "Free Fallin." It took a lot of practice to make the transitions as quickly as I needed to because the song has a quick tempo.

It took me awhile to be able to pick and sing at the same time. Once I could, I picked the verses and strummed the choruses. I added some dynamics and the song came together. This is one of the two songs I've spent the most time on, and yet I haven't played it for anyone, in large part because I feel I don't have it yet. After all, it's only been five years!

One of the hottest licks I've heard is when Billie Joe plays his acoustic version of the song at a concert in Japan. It's on YouTube and it lasts for 10 seconds starting at 1:28.[3] I've tried to figure out exactly how he does it. If anyone can figure out what he's doing, I'm all ears. It sounds like he may be alternating between picking muted notes and non-muted notes?

I'm disappointed I haven't been able to learn how to pick without looking. It's something I haven't worked on very much but I need to get a better feel for skipping strings without looking when I use a pick. I would like to fingerpick this song because it's more organic and easier than using a pick but I can also hear the dead notes because they are more pronounced. Which begs the question: Do professional guitarists ever miss a chord or a note? You really can't tell when bands are playing because other instruments cover up small mistakes. However, I have heard professionals hit a dead note. This usually occurs when they play fingerstyle on an acoustic. It's usually a slight miss though, and their mistakes don't really make a difference in the song.

If someone asked me to play a song, this would be one of my first choices. However, I recently let go of it because there's only so many times you can play a song before it gets old. It's better to put it on the back burner and come back to it later. Which begs the question, how do artists play the same songs night after night for 20 or 30 years? They must be sick of some of their songs, although I read that some artists enjoy playing certain songs every night. I wonder how Mick Jagger feels singing "Satisfaction" or "Jumpin' Jack Flash" for the 10,000th time. Perhaps the energy he expends on the stage helps get his adrenaline going?

The next song I wanted to learn was Bon Jovi's "Wanted Dead or Alive." I watched Bon Jovi and Richie Sambora perform it on MTV Unplugged in 1997 and their performance knocked me out. I never forgot it and I couldn't wait to learn how to play it when I bought my first guitar. It's another song that uses Cadd9 to G. I practiced it almost every day for a year. I got to the point where I could play it, although I couldn't do the opening lick as quickly as they could (and I don't even attempt the solo). But it still sounds awesome. The first time I was able to play the opening lick, I said to myself, "Move over Sambora!" HA! So even though I can't play it at the correct tempo, it's good enough for me. After all, who cares, right? It's not like I'm going to be headlining at Red Rocks.

I knew I was on the right path after I learned my first three songs. It gave me confidence that I could play any song if I practiced enough. However, I was incorrect because some songs were out of reach for me since I physically could not make the stretches some chords require. Given that I have a graduate degree in Education, you would think I would be intelligent enough to learn theory so I could find alternative chord shapes for those difficult chords. Sadly, that was not the case. I took the easy way out. I went to chorderator.com, a great online resource where I could get alternative fingerings for those difficult chords.

My problem with barre chords is that with my limited mobility I cannot get my thumb behind my fretted finger because it's always at a strange angle. I injured it by trying. Since I cannot fully supinate my wrist, I've found some success by swinging the neck of the guitar away from my body and leaning over so I can use the bonier side of my index finger to barre with.

The major challenge for me is the D barre chord shape. I cannot spread my first and third fingers enough to place them on the fifth and seventh frets. Barre chords are difficult enough for beginners, but immobility and small hands add to the challenge. I recently started doing wrist curls with a five-pound dumbbell to build strength in my wrist and forearms so hopefully that will help. I thought about placing small objects between my fingers and leaving them there for awhile for a gentle stretch, but when I tried it for a couple of minutes my fingers were sore. I didn't want to injure myself because tendons are delicate and connective tissue is fragile. I probably wouldn't think twice about it if I was 20 years old, but one of my goals is to prevent injuries.

Another goal is to incorporate percussive effects, or a cajon, a percussive instrument consisting of a wooden box with an attached kick pedal. This will open up possibilities for me. The more tools I have, the more creative I can be, so I began learning percussive effects like muting and palm slapping. It feeds my creative juices and that's when guitarists feel most alive, completely letting go and letting the creative process take over. It's fun to play songs but they are structured. The most enjoyment I get from guitar is when there are no expectations so I can create and explore. There is nothing like it.

Around the same time, I watched a friend of mine play a small gig. He was halfway through his first song when the song suddenly exploded. I hadn't noticed that he had a cajon. It was extremely effective. I was excited because my goal was to be able to control a snare drum and bass drum with my feet. I asked a veteran guitarist if he could maintain a simple drumbeat with his feet while playing guitar. His answer was, "No way." That scared me a little bit, but for some reason I believed I could do it. This belief was reinforced when I sat down at my electronic drum set with my guitar. I used a simple strumming pattern, basic chords, and a straightforward drumbeat, and after a few minutes I was able to do it.

FOR ME, playing acoustic guitar is all about strumming. Interestingly, I've discovered a difference in strumming patterns between someone who learns guitar via online tutorials compared to someone who learned how to play guitar by listening to albums and playing along with them during the pre-Internet days. Guitarists who learned to play by ear (i.e., before the Internet existed) have a huge advantage because their musical ear is more developed and they don't rely on preset strumming patterns like I did. They organically strum to match the rhythm of the song because that's how they learned. I've since learned how to do this but early on I spent a great deal of time memorizing strumming patterns. For instance, one pattern might be something like DDD DUDU DUDU, with D representing downstroke and U representing upstroke. For those who don't play guitar, this strumming pattern can sound completely different depending on dynamics (i.e., how loud or soft the notes are played). For example, an accent could be played on the first count; that is, the first note is louder to offset the next three notes. Variability in strumming patterns depends on the placement of accents. Using accents makes the song more pleasing to the ear by giving it a pattern. In contrast, if strings were hit with the same force every time throughout the song, it might get repetitive.

Muscle memory is remarkable. The human body can instantaneously move fingers to new positions for chord changes. When I strum fast, it doesn't leave much time to switch chords. There are little tricks, like eliminating the last strum to give you a little extra time or, if applicable, using one or more fingers as an anchor. I've also found that many acoustic songs tend to sound better if the last strum before a chord change is an upstroke.

People who don't play guitar may not be aware of "ghost strokes." It might look as though guitar players hit strings on every downstroke and upstroke. But that is not the case. Even though the hand might be continuously moving up and down, some strokes (or a lot, depending on the song and strumming pattern) miss the strings entirely. This gives the song rhythm, which makes it more pleasing to the ear. Additionally, guitar players do not always hit all six strings when they strum. For instance, they might hit only the bottom four strings (for D), or the bottom five strings (for C). When I began playing, I couldn't believe guitar players were that good, to be able to hit only a certain number of strings. However, it's nothing more than muscle memory, and all it takes is practice.

Another aspect I initially struggled with was trying to follow chord changes. I didn't have time to complete the full strumming pattern for each chord before I was supposed to switch chords. I might've been halfway through a strumming pattern when I changed chords, so was I supposed to finish the second half of the strumming pattern on the new chord, or begin the strumming pattern all over again on the new chord? This all sorted itself out in time.

Strumming was also a challenge because I had to strum left-handed and I'm not left-handed. It took me two years (!) to feel comfortable strumming. I'm grateful I didn't give up because strumming is now my favorite thing to do on my acoustic.

Initially, it was difficult to practice for a sustained period of time because I needed to build calluses on my fingertips. I had to take a day off but I tried to play through it. Eventually, within a few weeks I was able to develop calluses and can now play as long as I want. Although, there are times my fingertips might get a little sore if I'm using a capo on the fourth or fifth fret or higher. Early on, I purchased some rubber fingertips but it was impossible to play with them. And even though some people use Super Glue, I didn't try it because I was afraid I wouldn't be able to remove it.

Any new chord slowed me down when I began playing. That is, I could not transition from chord-to-chord quickly enough to play a song. There are two schools of thought in terms of how to get over this hump. First, don't slow down. That is, even if you don't have time to move your fingers into the correct position to play the chords perfectly, go ahead and maintain tempo. The second option is to play at a slower tempo so you have time to move your fingers into the correct position. The idea is that you can slowly increase the speed of the song as you improve until you reach the point where you can maintain tempo. I tried both methods and found that the latter method works better for me. Occasionally it doesn't, so I try the other method.

As of this writing, I've been playing for five years and it has not been easy. One has to be into delayed gratification to learn how to play guitar. It cannot be learned overnight and at this point I thought I would be better than I am. My issues with immobility can be frustrating and test my patience. I thought by now I would be a "real guitar player," whatever that means. A friend recently told me, "You're a guitar player," and my immediate reaction was, "No, I'm not." However, given my belief that we are what we do, and I play a couple of hours every day, maybe I am a guitar player. Just not a very good one. But I'll take it.

It's difficult to see daily progress, but the progress is clear-cut when I look at weeks or months. My only regret is that I didn't start playing when I was a kid. Sometimes, I am slow on the learning curve. For instance, in my 20s an ex-girlfriend told me she was attracted to every guy who had a guitar on his back. Somehow that escaped me. Certainly, if I could go back and spend my life on one hobby, it would be guitar.

I can't imagine how much I could've used my guitar when I was a teacher. I've seen teachers integrate music into the learning process with excellent results. I could've created song lyrics related to math, making it easier for students to remember terminology, processes, or equations. It would have been easy to do and fun for students. Not only that, a guitar can have a huge impact on classroom management. When students can't settle down, teachers notice an immediate impact as soon as they start playing guitar or any musical instrument. One secret is to include the students' names in songs. I've seen people do this and students get a kick out of it.

CHAPTER FOUR

A NEW WORLD

"Music is what tells us that the human race is greater than we realize."[1] Napoléon Bonaparte

A FRIEND TOLD me about alternative tunings two years after I started playing. It opened a new world for me. So that's how Jimmy Page was able to produce such haunting sounds on his acoustic! Alternative tunings sound more pleasant to my ear, perhaps because it's different than the standard tuning I've been playing in for so long. Truly, the most beautiful chords I've heard are in alternative tunings. My favorite chord in any tuning is Ano5/C# in DADGAD, used by Jimmy Page in "Kashmir." So far I've used DADGAD, CGDGBD, DADF#AD, DGCGCD, Open E, and Open A. Some chords sound huge in alternative tunings. For instance, I play Dave Mason's "We Just Disagree" in Open E because it sounds big and deep.

One benefit to alternative tunings is they are easier to play because some chords can be played with one or two fingers. So for someone with mobility issues, alternative tunings are perfect. For this reason, after playing covers for two years, I started writing my own songs using alternative tunings. The advantage to singing my own songs is I don't have to sound like other singers. I can make the song my own because it is. Plus I can match my voice to the key I play in.

I know the type of song I'm looking for. Take the song "Younger" by *A Great Big World*. It's a catchy, upbeat pop song with a great chorus that makes me feel good. This is the type of music I want to create.

The ultimate challenge is to see if I can write good songs. I've written ten songs but have yet to record them (more on this later). I can handle rhythm guitar, keyboards (very basic, but that's all I would need to get the "juice"), and drums. I'll need to hire someone to play bass, and perhaps a singer as well. It doesn't help matters that I don't know much music theory, but there have been plenty of songs written by people who don't know theory.

What does it take to write a good song? In addition to lyrics that tell a story, most songs have an intro, verses, a chorus, a bridge, and an outro. Some songs might have a pre-chorus. In my limited songwriting experience, I'm focusing on creating choruses that are easy to remember and sing along to. I'm trying to write choruses that are short, simple, and catchy.

Many songs are created by accident, which goes to show the serendipity involved in songwriting. No one can predict if a song is going to connect with the public. How many times have we heard of famous musicians who didn't think a particular song would make the album, let alone be a hit? One example is Kansas's "Dust in the Wind." One of the band members happened to be working on a riff at home on his acoustic. His wife thought he should play it for the band. He did, and the band knew it was going to be a hit.[2] Or take "Rock Candy" from Montrose's debut album. The drummer started laying down a heavy beat, Montrose came in with a riff on guitar, and Sammy Hagar made up some lyrics off the top of his head. Just like that, they had the genesis for a great rock song.[3]

Serendipity also plays a factor in song titles. For example, Sammy Hagar was once pulled over on a highway because he was clocked at 62 miles per hour. Hagar told the policeman, "I can't drive 55," and the song's title was born.[3]

Likewise, consider "American Woman" by The Guess Who. In Randy Bachman's autobiography, he explained how he'd been messing around with a riff for some time. He started playing it for the audience during a break at one of their shows. Singer Levon Helm got up to the mic and off-the-top of his head came up with the first line of the song. They continued exploring the song and that's how it came together.[4] And by the way, the B-side to "American Woman" was "No Sugar Tonight." That's right, two of the most iconic and popular songs from that generation on one single for approximately $1.00 back in 1970. As of this writing, it's available on Amazon.com for $6.00.

IF YOU WROTE A SONG, what would it be about?

Songland premiered on network television in 2019. It is an in-depth look at songwriting and a fast-track for singer-songwriters to get national attention. I couldn't wait to watch the show each week. Three celebrity producers work with amateur artists to improve their original songs. There is ample discussion about the songwriting process. Celebrity artists then choose the best song to record for their next album.

I'd love to see a show where the *minimum* age requirement is 50 years old. I understand the music industry is always looking for the next young star, but it would be nice to have more balance. I'm sure there are plenty of artists over 50 who have written great songs. Given the life experience older artists have, their lyrics might connect with the public. However, perhaps television producers believe older artists can't be idols and sell records unless they are already established and have a following? After all, the largest segment of consumers who purchase music are adolescents and millennial's, so perhaps the music industry believes the younger generation won't purchase music created by an older generation. However, if older artists had as much exposure as younger artists, I believe their music would sell, assuming the songs were as good as the songs created by younger artists. But what do I know, I'm just an old coot playing songs at home.

The best song I heard on *Songland* during the first season was "Pity Party." I told my wife it was a hit single, and yet incredulously it was not selected in the top three (out of four!). I went online and found other people saying the same thing. The same situation occurred during the second season when "That's a Country Song" was not chosen among the top three. I couldn't believe it. It was an anthem song and a potential monster hit. It made me wonder if the producers have the rights to sign artists from the show. I would love to invest in some of the artists. I'd like to see a mechanism whereby the public could invest in artists. Whether on *Songland* or *Shark Tank,* I believe there are many people who would jump at the opportunity to invest in songwriters or entrepreneurs.

CHAPTER FIVE

BACK TO THE WOODSHED

"One good thing about music, when it hits you, you feel no pain."[1] Bob Marley

A STUDENT WALKED into my office one day and told me her boyfriend was a guitar player, currently in a recording studio in Southern California with a big band. I asked her who the band was but she didn't know, so she texted him and found out it was the Foo Fighters. A few weeks later her boyfriend was in town so she invited me to watch him play. He played two of his original songs and I couldn't get them out of my head. I thought both were hit singles.

He was in town a few months later so I went over to see him. I told him there was an open mic that night at a local venue, so we headed over and he signed up to play. When his name was called, he walked up to the stage with a broken B-string, and he'd had a few beers. He borrowed someone's guitar and proceeded to play a cover of "Time to Pretend" by MGMT. He absolutely killed the song. I couldn't believe what I was watching. I don't drink, but my coordination would be way off if I drank several beers and I wouldn't be able to play guitar nearly as well. It made me wonder how rock stars can play under the influence. Perhaps because they practice that way? I do know the mind somehow remembers the state it is in. In other words, if you drink coffee to stay up all night to study for a final exam, then your results will be better if you drink coffee before you actually take the exam. Likewise, if you have a habit of playing guitar while under the influence, then you are probably going to be able to play guitar when you're under the influence.

But that is not all to the story. This happened to be Halloween and he was going out to party. We agreed he would come to my house the next morning to give me a guitar lesson. I wanted to get him on videotape so I could study the tape to learn. He showed up at 10:30 in the morning after only a few hours' sleep and said, "It was a pretty wild night." He then played a few songs. Somehow, he nailed the songs, even with little sleep, no more than a few bites of food the previous 24 hours, and a missing B-string on his guitar. In other words, a true rock star. When he needed to pick the B-string, he used his voice to mimic the sound that his B-string would have made. I guess this is what guitarists can do when they start playing at 10-years-old and have played half their life.

A few months later he was back in town. I showed him the theater at the local university. It was nighttime and it was raining, but the door was unlocked so we strolled in. He played a few songs on stage and I videotaped him, just in case he became famous he could sell his "basement tapes." What a treat it was for me to watch him up on stage in the theater playing his songs. At one point during the evening, he told me the two most important words of guitar advice I ever heard. When I told him I was practicing about an hour a day but it just wasn't happening, his reply was "play more." I suddenly realized he was in his 20s and played several hours a day, sometimes most of the day. Instructors had told me to play at least 20 minutes a day, so I thought I was putting in enough time to maximize my skills. However, I had to up my game so I started playing two hours or more a day. Indeed, I started noticing more improvement.

After he told me to play more, I began thinking about the best advice I've received in my life. I couldn't think of any specific advice but it occurred to me the most important lesson I've learned is forgiveness. I learned it from a young adolescent who had been bullied by several classmates. When a meeting was held to confront and discuss the situation, the student said, "I forgive you." Just like that. If only adults could forgive that quickly, I thought. I think about that lesson often when I need to forgive a friend or myself. It has saved me from a lot of internal turmoil, which, over time, can cause physical distress and even disease. So, I ask you, what is the most important lesson you've learned in your life?

Once I started practicing two hours a day, I began to get concerned that I could injure my arm or wrist if I strummed chords on my acoustic for that length of time. As it turned out, there were a handful of days where I was a little sore, but it hasn't been an issue. I feel blessed that I can play every day. Moreover, the law of diminishing returns comes into play when I practice for more than two hours at a time. On one hand, I think it's good to play for a long period of time because it increases my concentration span. Consequently, sometimes I'll leave my most difficult songs for the end of my session. It's the ultimate challenge. On the other hand, I'm not nearly as good after a couple of hours as I am first thing in the morning when I'm fresh. So it's a continual balancing act. The longest I've ever played at one time is three hours, although an hour and a half seems just right. Ideally, I would like to practice twice a day because repetition is critical and learning will be increased if I do something twice a day compared to once. It seems logical that if I practice twice a day I will improve twice as fast. Interestingly, (depending on the source) the human attention span is 10-

25 minutes, so I'm way over. One instructor told me it was a waste of time if I played for more than 20 minutes. However, sometimes if I practice for a couple of hours in the morning and then try to get back to it in the afternoon, I still feel burned out from the morning session. Why? Because when I play, I have to concentrate every single second. I'm not good enough to "mail it in."

As I stated earlier, who knows where I would be now if I started playing at a young age. I can't imagine having 50 years of guitar under my belt. I probably would have played in bands, the ultimate dream. It's difficult to find people to play with at my age, especially considering the type of music I want to play, which is classic songs from the 1960s and 1970s as well as some of the newer rock and pop songs. I'm also not good enough to learn unfamiliar songs quickly enough, unless it's a simple song using only major and minor open chords. I need time to practice songs so I feel confident enough to play them.

I love to practice. When I go to bed at night, I'm looking forward to playing the next morning. On top of that, I create new neurons in my brain when I play due to the multitasking involved. Sometimes I simultaneously read tabs, pick or strum, maintain tempo, add dynamics, and sing. In other words, the neurons in my brain are firing.

One mistake I made was wasting time when I began playing, because I practiced songs that were too difficult for me. I didn't have the skills yet but thought I would eventually acquire those skills if I kept practicing. If I could do it all over again, I would practice the major and minor open chords until I could easily transition from one to another. That is how you learn how to play songs, at least for a beginner. I also spent too much time practicing scales, which are not a waste of time, but I could've been using my time more wisely.

Another way I wasted time was trying to learn two instruments at once. For instance, I wanted to learn the piano introduction to Coldplay's "Fix You." I also spent some time learning the intro lick on drums because my idea was to combine the guitar, piano, and drums to see if I could replicate the song (without the vocals of course, because Chris Martin is one of those iconic singers). I'd never played keyboards before but there are YouTube tutorials that show the piano keys to play. I learned the introduction, although it wasn't complete because I used only one hand. Learning with both hands would have required too much time. It took me a few days to get it down but I never put the song together because I got tired of it. Since it's been three years, I've completely forgotten how to play it.

While I'm on the topic of keyboards, I recently learned the keyboard lick to Taylor Swift's "Miss Americana and the Heartbreak Prince." Now, you may be thinking, "Why is a 63-year-old guy learning a Taylor Swift song?" Well, it's because I like the melody. Similar to "Fix You," I want to combine the guitar, keyboard, and drum parts just to see if I can do it. Again, I'm using only one hand on the piano, but the piano riff gives the song the juice.

It's interesting how often the bass guitar or the "keys" stand out in songs. Sly and the Family Stone would not have reached the heights they did without their funky bassline. Likewise, there are many songs where keys make the song come alive. For instance, I watched a Bruno Mars interview on television where he described how he wrote "24K Magic." After he explained how he arranged the song, he walked over to the keyboard and said, "Then you add the sauce, the secret sauce."[2] He then hit a few keys and suddenly the song turned into one of the best dancing songs I ever heard.

AFTER I PLAYED for three years, a friend and I started getting together a couple of times a month to play. I immediately discovered I couldn't transition from chord-to-chord quickly enough to play most songs. I'd been playing songs by then but at a slower tempo, which allowed me an extra millisecond to get my fingers in the correct position. I also chose songs without barre chords, which meant that I didn't play any song that had F or B in the progression. What a huge mistake that was. It set me back and hindered my development.

I also learned how difficult it was to stay in time when I played with someone. This is a common occurrence when people start playing together, but I was surprised because I played drums for a short while decades ago and I thought I had a good sense of time. However, when I used a metronome, I discovered I had a tendency to play too fast. So here I was, a rhythm guitar player who purposely stayed away from barre chords and played too fast. Those are bad traits for a guitar player. I changed my practice routine to focus on five or six songs that we played. It took me a few months to get to the point where I could play those songs in time, in large part due to the prevalence of F#m in several of the songs. For someone with mobility issues, that chord is a monster. No matter how I position my index finger when I barre the second fret, I cannot push the G string down hard enough to play a clean chord. Due to my immobility, I cannot roll my index finger to use the side of it (where it's bonier) because if I do that I cannot extend my third and fourth fingers to the fourth fret. I've been working on the following progression for awhile and I still have difficulty playing it at only 90 bpm: F#m/Bm/F#m/C#m/F#m. Back to the woodshed, I guess.

Before I played with my friend, musicians told me the quickest way to improve was to play with another person. How right they were.

CHAPTER SIX

PRIORITIES

"Everything is hard before it is easy."[1] Goethe J.W.

BEFORE I RETIRED, I tried to squeeze in 15 or 30 minutes of practice before driving to work, a 45 minute commute. It killed me that I had to waste time driving when I could've been playing. The more I improved, the more I didn't want to go to work. There were days when I was dialed in and suddenly I had to leave for work. Sometimes I had barely warmed up. It was frustrating. I knew I needed to retire as soon as it was financially viable because my job was getting in the way of my playing. Priorities, right?

According to a theory posited by author Malcolm Gladwell, it requires 10,000 hours to master something.[2] I've played an average of two hours a day for five years, so I'm at 3,650 hours or about 37% toward mastering the instrument. Of course I won't get there because of my limited mobility, but it's all about the process. I would be happy simply mastering some of my favorite songs and being able to solo a little bit. This is what I tell myself whenever I get frustrated. I've been working on some songs for years that I still don't have down. It makes me wonder, "Am I an idiot for doing the same thing over and over again and expecting different results?" Or, if I keep at it, will I be able to play these songs at some point? As soon as I learn a new song and can play it (but not perfectly), I'm ready to move on because I want to be constantly learning. The trouble with this approach is I never really master any song. But I'm tired of the song because I spent so long practicing it. I have a friend who plays the same song 10 times in a row, but I can't do that. I play a song once, although I stop to work on parts that are difficult. Another reason I like to move on after learning a song is there's something inherently satisfying about learning a new song. I think it's the excitement of learning how to play some of the songs I grew up with. I feel like a rock star the first time I can play a new song.

Once I get sick of a song, it's out of my practice rotation for awhile. Then it's back in at some point, then out, then in again. I have about 140 songs and I can practice no more than 15-20 a day. Plus I need to give more time to the newer songs, which means it's difficult to get to some of the older songs. I know one thing for certain: I have to be the worst player on the planet who has put in so many hours. But who cares? I'm lucky to be able to play at all. It's an honor to pick up my guitar every day. I could never thank her enough for the enjoyment she has given me.

One of my roommates in college had a theory about his car. Sometimes his car did not start so he would leave it alone and come back a few days later to try again. Lo and behold, it would usually start. This theory seems to work well for me, because when I quit a difficult song and then come back to it a few months later, it's easier for me because my skills have improved.

I had to take a few days off to work on this book and that made me nervous, because I'm afraid my skills will deteriorate or I'll forget some of the songs. I start getting really concerned if I take two days off in a row. I took three days off once and it felt like eternity. However, I have a foundation built up and a couple of times I actually improved after I took a day off.

CHAPTER SEVEN

AND IT'S FREE

"Music is the fastest motivator in the world."[1] Amit Kalantri

ONCE I STARTED PLAYING GUITAR, I began listening to all the different instruments in a song. Prior to that, like most people who don't play an instrument, I listened to music purely for enjoyment. But now that I play an instrument, I don't want to waste any potential learning opportunities.

I've tried several instructors during the last five years. A couple of them were a little frustrated because I played left-handed and had mobility issues, so I quit because I could sense their frustration. One instructor kept taking calls on his cell phone during my lesson so I left. Another instructor was down-right condescending so I quit after one lesson. After three years, I discovered that if I videotape my instructor playing, then I could watch the tape over and over. I learn more using that method.

I struggle with anxiety when I play in front of someone. My guess is this came from my dad because I always wanted to please him. I was afraid when he asked me to help him work on our car or around the house because he would get angry if I did something wrong. I was full of anxiety and I have the same feeling today when I try to play in front of someone. Consequently, this is why I make mistakes when instructors ask me to play. Sometimes I feel like I'm killing it (relatively) when I play alone at home and I wish that my instructor could see me play that way. After five years, I've played in front of only two people for any length of time and both times I was extremely nervous. However, after a few minutes I was able to concentrate and my nerves dissipated, which told me that I need to play in front of people if I ever want to play publicly.

My first instructor had me practice the C major scale. I did that every day for a month and was bored to tears, although in hindsight that exercise helped me develop flexibility and strength in my fingers. It also exposed me to a bit of music theory because I had to read sheet music. Like many people starting out on a musical instrument, I did not like reading sheet music. I felt it slowed me down so I quit. Now, however, I regret not keeping at it. A friend of mine told me it was a two-year process for him to be able to play to sheet music. He told me he can now play songs immediately by reading the sheet music as he's playing. I can't imagine how good that would feel. Part of me says that I'm too old to learn now, but I know that's not true. Simply put, I don't want to put out the effort. My rationale is I can already play songs so there's no need for me to learn how to read sheet music.

I also took two lessons from a classical guitarist. He had me set the body of the guitar in between my thighs with the neck almost straight up, playing fingerstyle. This is considered proper technique and will minimize injuries over the long run. Indeed, it was easier for me to form the chord shapes with my fingers using that set up, but the problem was I couldn't strum because the neck was almost vertical. That was a major problem because I love strumming. I'm also not interested in playing classical style where most of the notes are picked individually. Plus, I think there's a certain amount of vanity involved because I wanted to at least look like a guitar player. I didn't want to be playing Green Day or Led Zeppelin songs using the posture of a classical guitarist.

My first instructor taught me an advanced strumming pattern that involved dynamics. I practiced it every day for two months and could never get it. Then I started taking lessons from a flamingo player who taught me fingerstyle. After the first lesson, I came home and practiced finger style for 15 or 20 minutes. Then I tried the strumming pattern with a pick and suddenly I was able to do it. Something had clicked in my mind-body connection, and fingerstyle made it easier for me to strum with a pick. This led to the realization that every little thing I learn on guitar adds to my skills, whether it's scales, soloing, fingerstyle, strumming, playing chords, finger tapping, or playing up the fretboard.

One instructor taught me the major and minor pentatonic scales. Another taught me the CAGED system. A third instructor taught me the C and G major and minor "runs." Another instructor taught me the A blues scale in minor pentatonic and the C major pentatonic scale. I felt I had enough of a foundation to move on. Amazingly, I've never used any scales in the songs I play because I don't solo. However, scales helped me to build strength and dexterity in my fingers, and made me more comfortable playing up and down the fretboard.

One day I learned a lick from YouTube and then didn't play it for a few days. I subsequently forgot the lick and the song. This brings up the conundrum of how to maximize practice to get the most return. One of my instructors told me to split my practice time into thirds: Work on old material, work on new material, and have fun. The gentleman I bought my first guitar from told me when he was a kid he practiced four chords all summer long: G, C, D, and Em. He had those chords down, but that is not the way to inspire a beginning guitarist. However, he stuck with it and now owns his own music store.

Another instructor showed me his foot pedals. It was fascinating to hear the different sounds foot pedals can make. Pedals can be used with acoustic guitars, although the effect is not as pronounced as it is with electrics. I bought several pedals: Dunlop Wah Wah, Digitech Grunge, Danelectro Phaser, Danelectro Overdrive, and Digitech Multi-Effects. I felt like Hendrix at Woodstock when I hooked them up. I played for a few minutes with each one but it wasn't as exciting as I thought it would be, mostly because I played acoustic. That said, the Wah Wah did sound wicked, but I haven't used it for a couple of years. My guess is there aren't many people in their 60s who play for fun at home who use pedals with their acoustic.

My best instructor has been YouTube. And it's free. If I was forced to choose only one website to visit for the rest of my life, it would be YouTube. I've learned a lot, not only from tutorials but also from people who play covers.

For example, in May 2020 I found a YouTube video of Katy Perry giving a guitar lesson for her new single "Daisies." (I believe it has since been taken down because I can't find it). In full disclosure, Perry's music is a guilty pleasure for me. I love some of her songs. Songs like "Wide Awake" and "Teenage Dream" are incredibly catchy. The melodies she creates are so powerful that I can't get them out of my head for days. There's something about her voice that resonates with me when she goes into her falsetto at the end of a verse or chorus. For instance, listen to the outro of "Wide Awake," or the notes she hits during the last "daisy" in the last chorus of "Daisies." I love the pitch of her voice when she does this. So you can imagine how I felt when I found a video of her giving a guitar lesson on "Daisies." It's a simple three-chord song and she gave an inspirational, positive lesson. If millions of adolescent girls knew this video existed, perhaps some would want to emulate their idol and learn how to play guitar. It could change their lives.

I also found a YouTube tutorial featuring Alex Lifeson (guitarist for Rush) demonstrating one of his songs.[2] It's amazing to learn from the rock star who actually created the song. I was surprised by his teaching skills. He was methodical, progressed at a rate that even a beginner can follow, and used repetition. But what stood out is how humble he was. Here's a major rock star giving a tutorial and he comes across as just another guy. Which he is, of course.

One of the most astonishing videos I've watched on YouTube is a guy (playguitarsolos.com) who plays the solo from "I'd Love to Change the World."[3] He knocks it out of the ballpark note for note, replicating the tone and feel of the original. My instructor asked me if I'd like to learn it. I had to laugh because it would take me a lifetime to learn that solo. But a guy can always dream. The other astonishing YouTube video I've seen is Johnny A playing "Wichita Lineman."[4] I've never heard a more beautiful rendition of any song played on an electric guitar.

There are many instructors on YouTube who have helped me. My favorite is Marty Schwartz. He is an excellent teacher, as are the instructors from Shut up and Play, Andy Guitar, Justin Guitar, Country Song Teacher, Learn Guitar Favorites, Papastache Pop, Guitar Lessons 365, and Rick Beato, who conducts something akin to a master class. He breaks songs down and explains the music theory behind them. He is an amazing resource to learn from. In one of his videos, he plays the top 20 intros of all time on acoustic guitar.[5] This is something I'm interested in because I like playing intros.

I can't say enough about the learning opportunities on YouTube. There's one video of a young woman playing a cover of Tears for Fears' "Everybody Wants to Rule the World."[6] I've been working on that song for three years, but she plays it better than me. And I'm willing to bet she didn't need to practice it for three years. But who cares? If I keep practicing a song for months, I can get to a point where I'm comfortable with it. I just don't want to embarrass myself. After all, my guess is there are millions of people who are much better players and singers than I am. So what? This is not a competition. I've heard stories of guitarists jamming and it turns into a competition. That is not what it's about. It's about having fun, self-expression, making connections, and touching people with music. I can't think of a better legacy. We are all on different paths and it's unfair to compare our paths with anyone else. I am working to be the best that I can be and that's good enough. That said, I'm definitely intimidated to play in a music store because I'm probably the worst player in the store. Sometimes I'll see young kids killing it and it can be a little demoralizing. But can they sing, play rhythm, keep the tempo, and write their own songs?

Speaking of music stores, one thing I've learned is there are some riffs that should not be played in the stores because they have been overplayed and owners are sick of hearing them. They include "Layla," "Stairway to Heaven," "Smoke on the Water," "Smells Like Teen Spirit," "Sweet Child O' Mine," "Sweet Home Alabama," "Back In Black," "Enter Sandman," and Eddie Van Halen's finger tapping from "Eruption," among others.

Sometimes I'm inspired by artists on YouTube. Other times, I'm intimidated. Or perhaps both at the same time. Consider Gabriella Quevedo, a finger style player who plays covers of rock and pop songs. In one video, she plays Aerosmith's "Dream On," and it's gorgeous. She used two capos at once, something I'd never seen before. Even more impressive is the fact she played this song when she was 18 years old, after playing for only six years.[7] In another video, Bruce Springsteen invited a young fan to join him on stage to play "Growin' Up."[8] The kid pulled it off, no doubt the greatest day of his life.

Could I do that? I don't know, but if I could have one wish related to music, that would be it.

Almost every song I've learned has been from YouTube and ultimate-guitar.com. My process is this: I go to ultimate-guitar.com to get the lyrics and the chords for the song I want to learn. Then I go to YouTube to see if anybody has uploaded a lesson on it. Usually, somebody has. If not, I check to see if there are any covers of the song. This gives me a good idea of the strumming pattern, which is critical to get the rhythm of the song. I'm at the point now where I can make up strumming patterns but early on it was my most prevalent question. Viewers agree, because if you look at the comments below tutorials, many beginning players ask about the strumming pattern. Once I played for awhile, I discovered I can use the same strumming pattern for almost any song. It's all in the dynamics. Simply using an accent on the first count seems to work most of the time.

Speaking of ultimate-guitar.com, it is a wonderful resource for musicians. Type in the song you want to learn and there are usually (but not always) people who have posted their versions of the songs with tabs or chords. I didn't play guitar before the Internet existed but it used to be that musicians had to listen to records over and over again to learn how to play songs. They had to keep lifting the arm of the turntable and setting it down again on the same part. It was a more organic way to learn how to play. Now it's convenient because the chords are posted online.

In addition to learning songs on YouTube, I've also learned techniques like bends (bending strings), vibrato (slightly bending a note so the pitch moves to and fro), slides (sliding from one fret to another while pressing down on one or more strings), hammer-ons (plucking one or more strings and immediately "hammering" one or more fingers down on them), and harmonics (lightly touching strings just prior to picking or strumming them and then immediately releasing the strings). These techniques give me additional tools to work with and can take a song to the next level. When I combine these techniques with muting, fingerstyle, dynamics, percussive effects, and a capo, the possibilities are endless.

It's easy to get lost on YouTube. Occasionally I find myself watching videos, when what I really want to be doing is playing. For instance, I'll suddenly realize I've been watching carpool karaoke for an hour or so. It's must-see for music lovers, where some of the most famous musicians in the world sing in a car. Whoever came up with that concept was brilliant. My favorite episodes include Paul McCartney, Adele, Lady Gaga, and Chris Martin, as well as one episode with Gwen Stephani, Julie Roberts, and George Clooney. The McCartney segment stands out because he's driven to his old house, and later in the segment he surprises patrons in a pub by playing several of his songs. Goosebumps.

CHAPTER EIGHT

FIVE YEARS?

"If I cannot fly, let me sing."[1] Stephen Sondheim

WHAT'S your first memory of singing?

I don't have one. I never sang in my life before I started playing guitar, not even in the shower or my car. This is in stark contrast to Roger Daltrey, who reminisced in his autobiography about how common it was for people to sing in public areas when he was growing up. He told a story of working in a factory as a young man. The employees used raw materials that were lying around to make drum sounds so they could engage in sing-alongs to a beat.[2]

How often do factories in America give their employees time for sing-alongs? If employers want to increase productivity in the workplace, all they have to do is have breaks for sing-alongs. The productivity would increase because singing would help employees bond with each other and they would be happier. Not only is this common sense, but studies indicate there is an association between singing and its effect on the immune system.[3] Studies also indicate heart rates sync in alignment when people sing.[4] Wow! In other words, music has the ability to increase or decrease heart rates so that everyone singing in a group has the same heart rate. This is absolutely mind-blowing and confirms how music is profoundly embedded in our hearts. Perhaps this helps to explain the natural high singers feel when they sing in unison. After all, did the Beach Boys or Crosby, Stills, Nash and Young feel the natural high when they sang? You bet they did.

Daltrey also remembered people singing in the streets as they went about their business.[2] I can't remember the last time I was out in public and I heard somebody sing. It's unfortunate because with the Internet and televised singing competitions, I would think people would be singing in the streets throughout America.

A friend recently sent me some questions to reflect on my life. One of them was, "What would you choose to do if you couldn't fail?" My answer is sing. Singing has been a challenge for me. I wanted to be able to sing songs and play for people, so I took five singing lessons after I played for a year. I learned the correct posture, how to move from my chest voice to my head voice, how to breathe properly, and how to control my diaphragm. I concentrated on taking a breath at the beginning of every sentence or phrase in a song. If I didn't, I could run out of air. Sometimes I thought more about breathing than singing or playing. Perhaps I haven't done it enough for it to become second nature. A singer told me, "Just sing, don't think." That is good advice because I have a tendency to overthink things. Sometimes I'll practice the "do re mi fa so la ti do" scale, and try to use those pitches when I sing. Another thing I learned is that it's not easy to project a falsetto. This is why Adam Levine is so good at what he does. He can project his falsetto.

I am not alone with the challenge of singing. In this day and age of mediocrity, there are plenty of singers who sing out of key or scream lyrics on television shows like *American Idol* or *The*

Voice. Every time a contestant starts screaming, the crowd responds. On one hand, people deserve support, but is it honest to shower singers with platitudes when they don't deserve it? Perhaps the audience is told when to respond, I don't know. Furthermore, when a judge offers constructive criticism that is warranted, the audience will boo. It's all part of our politically-correct culture where if you disapprove, you are criticized or called a "hater."

Some of my favorite singers include Jewel, Alicia Keys, Ann Wilson (Heart), Springsteen, Tom Johnston (The Doobie Brothers), Chris Martin (Coldplay), Tracy Thorne and Ben Watt (Everything but the Girl), and Stephen Jenkins (Third Eye Blind). Jenkins has a unique way of blending hip-hop rhythms into his songs. It's extraordinary catchy. He was the valedictorian for his class at the University Of California, where he majored in linguistics. He has an affinity with words and I believe he's one of the best songwriters.

A friend told me about recording software a year after I began singing. I was excited to record myself so I purchased a Shure Beta 58A microphone and a Scarlett 2i2 audio interface. I recorded one song and listened to it. I was horrified. I'd never heard anything so awful. The guitar sounded muffled, I couldn't stay in rhythm, and my voice sounded terrible. I thought, "What is the point of trying to do this if I can't at least sound decent enough to sing for friends? Is there any point to playing by myself day after day?" The answer is yes. It's about the journey and the joy; it's not about the end product.

Musicians told me my reaction was normal; that many people are disappointed the first time they hear themselves sing. Once I had practiced singing my original songs for a few months, a friend sang a couple of my songs. Within seconds, I realized I have a long way to go. Granted, she had been singing most of her life, but at this point I don't have any false hopes about becoming a good singer. And that's putting it mildly.

During one summer, I decided to play and sing the same three songs every day to see if I could eventually pull it off. The three songs I chose were "Fix You" by Coldplay, "I Can't Make You Love Me" by Bonnie Raitt, and "Good Riddance" by Green Day. After three months, my singing wasn't happening so I took a break. I was so sick of the songs I couldn't play them anymore. It's a challenge to play covers of well-known songs because the public knows them well and there are certain expectations. But I don't have a voice like Raitt, or Coldplay's Chris Martin, or Green Day's Billie Joe Armstrong, so I try to make each song my own. The most difficult songs for me to sing are songs where the singers talk their way through the song. I have tried repeatedly to mimic the cadence of Billie Joe in "Good Riddance" but it's difficult to do. Likewise, trying to imitate Rihanna's cadence in "Work" is an exercise in futility.

This reminds me of a situation when I told a friend I couldn't begin to sing "Crazy on You" by Heart. Ann Wilson sings that song in a higher key than me. My friend expressed surprise that I couldn't hold up to one of the most iconic female voices of all time. He was kidding of course, and I could only laugh. Why do I keep choosing songs by iconic singers? It's because they're great songs. In these situations, I end up singing softly or even talking my way through the lyrics. At least I eventually learn the lyrics that way.

While on the topic of lyrics, I met a 64-year-old man who told me he couldn't learn new songs because he couldn't remember lyrics. I felt a little better about singing because one challenge is trying to remember the lyrics from so many songs. Some people can sing the same songs over and over but I can't sing a song more than once a day. I'll sing a song once a day every day for a few months before I can remember the lyrics. But then I get tired of the song so I'll rotate it out of my setlist. When I come back to it months later, I've forgotten some of the lyrics. I wonder how often professional musicians forget lyrics, given that some artists have a catalog of hundreds of songs. Interestingly, I haven't noticed any singers forget lyrics during the concerts I've been to.

My guitar has a small body and therefore doesn't have as much volume as a larger-body guitar. This is why my guitar sounded muffled on my recording. At least that's what my instructor told me. Moreover, the sound was muffled because too much of the surface area of my pick touched the strings when I strummed. I needed to learn how to strum the strings lighter so only the tip of the pick touches the strings instead of digging in.

A musician told me I have to play to a "click track" so I can stay in tempo. What he meant was that I needed to play to a metronome and record that track. Then I could play along with that track because the timing would be correct. However, when I turned the metronome up high enough so I could hear it while singing and playing, it interfered with the recording. In addition, I couldn't hear the sound of the metronome in my headphones, as it wasn't coming through. A host of issues cropped up after that so I spent time troubleshooting. My next attempt wasn't much better. I had to turn the volume all the way up on my audio interface to get the volume of my guitar up to the level of the mic I used for my voice. I kept thinking, "Can I just pay somebody to do this for me?" Of course I could, if I ever get to the point where I can actually play my songs. However, that might get expensive because one of my instructors told me that when people come to his studio to record, they think they can record the song in one take. But it turns out they want to record it over and over to get it just right. It can be costly.

I quit recording myself and instead focused on constructing songs using prerecorded audio clips provided by the recording software. I constructed the songs digitally with the exception of some keyboards I played on my computer keyboard (try playing chords on a computer keyboard sometime). I couldn't use my

Yamaha keyboard because my CPU could not translate the digital sounds to analog quickly enough. An expert at Sweetwater told me it was a common problem with keyboards (especially synthesizers) and home computer systems.

My recording software included thousands of prerecorded audio clips from dozens of instruments. I began by clicking and dragging audio clips from the library onto a timeline. I was hooked! I was surprised at how easy it was to construct a song. If everybody knew how easy this was, they would be doing it. After I had a drumbeat, I started stacking other instruments on the timeline. Some of the clips sounded good and some didn't. After awhile, I got familiar with what worked and what didn't. I emailed the support team and used the manual when needed, but a lot of the learning process involved experimentation and troubleshooting. I solved problems by learning multiple ways to do things.

I enjoyed the challenge of trying to construct quality songs. I wanted to compose eight songs so I could call it a full album. I created 10 songs but the quality wasn't there, so I started combining songs. I finished with four songs.

One mistake I made was overthinking things and spending too much time on one song. After awhile, I questioned my judgment because objectivity gets lost after listening to a song so many times. This is common among artists during the recording process.

The next step was to create videos for my songs. I selected some video templates from a website a friend suggested. He put the templates together to create videos and uploaded them on YouTube under the name "Rainbow Annie."

Next, I tried recording drums and keyboards for my original songs. Everything worked and I was excited to begin putting songs together. That was a year ago but I still haven't done it because of the muffled sound from my guitar. I might need to get a guitar with more projection, I'm not sure. I also don't think

I'm good enough on the guitar yet to be recorded, although this might be my own insecurity talking. It's the ultimate delayed gratification: I'm not recording myself because I want to get to a certain point on the guitar to feel confident before I start recording. When will that be? It's been five years! Plenty of musicians post their songs on YouTube after only a few months of playing. But five years? Who knows if I'll ever get to the point where I feel confident enough to post my original songs online. The first step is finding a left-handed acoustic guitar with a 1.75 nut width (more on this later) and more projection than the guitar I currently play with. I've been meaning to take a trip to the San Francisco Bay Area to look for a new guitar, but as I write this we are in the midst of the COVID-19 pandemic so my trip has been postponed.

CHAPTER NINE

MY GIRL

"Music is the strongest form of magic."[1] Marilyn Manson

IF YOU ARE CONSIDERING TAKING up guitar, you don't need an expensive guitar to play and have fun. Actually, some of the best songs ever written have been played on cheap guitars. That said, it is more satisfying to play a decent guitar.

I played my first guitar (the previously mentioned Recording King) for six months before I graduated to a Taylor 210. What a difference in sound. However, the Taylor body was too big for me and it also has a 1 11/16 in. nut width, which is too narrow for me. (Nut width is the measurement across the top of the fret-board where the first fret begins. The smaller the measurement, the closer the strings are to each other). I need a wider nut width to give me more space in between the strings, because I cannot bend my knuckles enough to get my fingers in a vertical position to press down on the strings. The result is my fingers touch strings they should not be touching and thus I hit "dead" notes. I struggled with my Taylor for a year and then I graduated to a Martin 00-18VS, which was easier to play due to its low action and wider (1.75 in.) nut width. Amazingly, a 1.75 nut width is only .0625 wider compared to 1 11/16, but it's a huge difference in the way a guitar feels. I was ecstatic because I wasn't hitting dead notes anymore, plus the low action was easier on my arm. (For those who don't play guitar, low action occurs when the strings are close to the fretboard, thereby minimizing tension on the arm, wrist, and fingers). My Recording King and Taylor both had higher action, even though at that point I did not know what action was. Once I got my Martin, I was amazed at how much easier it was to play.

My Martin was inspired by the Unofficial Martin Guitar Group. The group came up with the design and specifications and Martin made 120 of them, with only one or two being left-handed. It's my little baby and has an amazing sound. It's also great for fingerstyle because of its wider nut width. My only problem is I often hear buzzing from strings touching the frets when I strum hard. This is because of the low action, which I need to save my arm. It's a trade-off; with higher action I could get a cleaner sound but it could potentially damage my arm in the long run.

I like the sound of an acoustic guitar compared to an electric. Acoustic guitars are also easier for me to play, which is the reason I own only one electric guitar. It's an Epiphone Special 2, a low-end model. I bought it from a college student for $50. Given that I hardly ever play electric guitar, it's good enough for me. The reason I don't play electric is because the neck is longer than an acoustic, and with my limited mobility it's almost impossible to play in the first position (i.e., at the far end of the fretboard). Since I have to have the neck of the guitar up toward my face, I need to use a guitar strap to pull it way up against my upper chest. This is the only way I can play in the first position but it's a challenge because the neck keeps slipping away from my body and I have trouble controlling it. Maybe I'm not used to it. After all, millions of people play electrics without a problem, but they don't have their guitars placed up high against their chest because they don't have a problem reaching the first position on the fretboard. I've tried to play my electric several times but each time I get frustrated. At this point, it's not like I'm going to be a shredder or play crazy solos, although if I could learn a couple of my favorite solos that would be good enough for me.

In terms of guitar strings, I use D'Addario Extra Lights "10s" or "11s" (i.e., the diameter of the thinnest string in thousandths of an inch, with the five other strings increasing progressively, so the thickest string might be .047 or .056 or .059). I usually use .010 - .047. The advantage to using light strings is they are thinner and therefore easier on the arm, wrist, and fingers. However, thin strings do not project as much as thicker strings but it saves my arm and helps me avoid injuries. I'll make that trade any day. Now, if I was a young man I'd probably be playing with 12s to get more projection. This might not seem like a big deal for people who don't play guitar but it's a huge change when I've been playing with 10s or 11s. The difference between the diameters of an .010 string compared to an .011 string is only one thousandth(!), while the difference in some of the thicker strings might be a few thousandths. But it makes all the difference in the world, because guitarists are intimately familiar with the feel of their guitars and strings. Given that many guitar players hold a guitar in their lap for hours every day, for years, their mind-body connection with the instrument is totally dialed in.

I've used phosphor bronze strings, 80/20 bronze, silk and steel, coated 80/20 bronze, nickel plated, and Elixirs. I've tried several brands but to me strings are similar to betting on the ponies. Instead of betting on a long shot, why not just select the heavy favorite? You won't get rich but you will lower your risk and mitigate losses. The same holds true for the stock market. Instead of trying to guess which stocks will yield the best return, why not just select the leader in an industry sector? The point I'm trying to make is that D'Addario is a leader in the music industry, so I stick with them. Furthermore, I can't tell the difference in the sound of different brands of strings because I leave my strings on my guitar for six months or so and the sound deteriorates so incrementally day-by-day that I'm used to it, so when I put new strings on they sound incredible, no matter the brand. Perhaps I would be able to tell the difference in sound between different brands and types of strings if I started playing as a kid and had more of a developed ear. The reason I don't change strings very often is because new strings are slippery and my fingers tend to slip off on certain chords because I cannot spread my fingers out. It's the result of the operation I had on my arm years ago. I tried Elixir strings once and I couldn't play anything because my fingers kept slipping off. It's too bad, because they are easier on fingers and more durable.

I also don't like to take time to change strings. It takes me a half-hour and I could be using that time to play. The same holds true for alternative tunings; I love to play in alternative tunings but I don't want to take the time to retune even though it takes less than 30 seconds or so, so I leave my guitar in whatever tuning I finished playing in that day, unless I've tuned one or more strings up. In that case I loosen them because an employee at Martin told me my guitar could be damaged if I left strings tuned up for a sustained period of time. When I pick up my guitar the next day, I don't want to immediately retune so I continue playing in that tuning. My concern is that I'm getting lazy playing in alternative tunings too much and therefore could be losing some of my skills playing in the first position in standard tuning. However, there's nothing worse than sitting down to play only to have to wait until I retune. Or clip my fingernails, which guitar players do often. When I want to play, I want to play. I mean, right now.

My dream guitar was a Gibson J45, until I heard a Guild D55.

The J45 is one of the most iconic guitars of all time. I'd actually like to get a Jumbo, but it's too expensive and the body might be too big for me because I play sitting down and it might be difficult to get my arm around. The J45 is a dreadnought, which might be difficult since I have to raise the neck up toward my head in order to play certain chords. Like I stated earlier, when I do this, the guitar has a tendency to slip off of my thigh. But I'll live.

The J45 is called "the workhorse" because it's been used extensively by professional musicians for decades. Supposedly, it's a good fit for the human voice, unlike some guitars that might have a tendency to dominate vocals. For instance, I was at a luthier one day when a customer brought in a Martin D28. I could not believe the projection from that guitar. I wanted one but I thought it might be too loud for my voice. Since I usually don't mic up or plug-in when I play at home, I need a guitar that blends well with my voice. The Guild D55 sounds fuller and deeper than the Gibson. The only problem is the Guild has a 1 11/16 nut width. If it was 1.75, I'd have one in my house right now. Likewise, I was in a music store once when an employee played a Yamaha TransAcoustic guitar. He set the guitar to electronic mode so it sounded like it was plugged in. It sounded amazing. Yamaha does not make a left-handed model or I would've bought it on the spot.

In 2016, I heard "Love Somebody" by St. Lucia. The song incorporated some cool sounds from a synthesizer and it had a deep bass drop that I wanted to use in my songs, so I purchased a Roland Juno synthesizer. I paid one of my instructors to show me how to operate it, but I didn't have the time to use it because I needed to focus my efforts on guitar. After a few months, I traded the synthesizer to my instructor for six months of lessons. Now, of course, I wish I still had it. How many musicians have regretted selling one of their guitars or instruments? There are plenty of guitarists who regret "letting that one go," often when they were young and struggling financially. I also have a Roland electronic drum set, a low-end Yamaha classical guitar, a Yamaha keyboard, a Fishman Loudbox acoustic amp, and the previously mentioned Taylor and Recording King guitars.

Guitar players have their favorite plectrums (i.e., guitar picks). Most guitarists hold a pick between their thumb and forefinger, unless they play fingerstyle. Players get used to holding picks a certain way because they hold them for thousands of hours over the course of years. Picks come in different shapes, sizes, material, and widths. When I started playing, I used a pick that was too stiff and it made it difficult for me to strum. Strumming was easier once I used a medium-size pic with a width of .6. Once I find a pic that I like, that's all I play with until I lose it, it wears out, or it breaks. It borders on superstition but I think it's a confidence factor because if I feel good with a pick in my fingers, then that's one less thing to worry about. However, after four years, I decided to change the way I held the pick. This change might seem trivial to those who don't play guitar, but it was significant for me because guitar is based on feel. I was using an oversize pick because I'm missing my middle finger on my strumming hand. I don't have complete feeling in my forefinger either, so I needed to put two fingers on the back of the pick for stability. However, this meant I couldn't fully use the hybrid picking technique (using a pick and fingers) because I only had my pinky to fingerpick with. So I changed to a normal-size pick and I'm using only my thumb and forefinger (like all other guitarists), so I have two fingers I can fingerpick with. This was a huge change because there's a different feel when I strum. It took me two months to get used to the change.

What's amazing about picks is how I lose so many of them. I have no idea where they go; sometimes my wife will find them in the laundry. Sometimes a pick will fly out of my hand when I'm playing and I can't find it. I know it's within three or four feet of me and yet there have been times when I can't find it.

One time I found a pick a couple feet away from me in between a couple of crevices on my kick pedal for my drum set. It had nudged its way into a small crack and it was almost impossible to see. They seem to have a life of their own. Sometimes I'll accidentally drop the pick into the sound hole of my guitar, so I turn the guitar upside down and shake it. My guess is every person who has ever played guitar has had this experience. After this happens a few times, you get pretty good at shaking the picks out of your guitar. That said, one time I couldn't get the pick out so I left it in my guitar. The next day I tried it again but the pick was no longer inside, or it had fastened itself to something inside the guitar. A couple of weeks later, it fell out.

Another change I made was to stop using a footrest, which raised my left leg up a few inches off the ground so my guitar rested on my thigh. This stabilized the guitar and prevented it from flopping around when I played. It was a comfortable position because my guitar rested in my lap and it was in my sweet spot. However, the footrest was a crutch so I quit using it. This also took me awhile to get used to. By the way, I always play sitting down even though I realize it would be healthier for my hips and back if I played standing up. Recently I played standing up for 20 minutes and I was beginning to get used to it, so I will do that more.

CHAPTER TEN

SETLIST

"I see my life in terms of music."[1] Albert Einstein

ONE OF THE great things about playing guitar is deciding which songs I want to learn. This is not easy because there are hundreds of songs I would like to be able to play. I might learn a new song in minutes or it might take me months, depending on the complexity of the song and the chord progression. So when I'm selecting new songs, it's important I do so judiciously.

Where do I get my songs? Many of them are from my younger days. I find current songs on YouTube or on television shows, especially music award shows. For instance, I heard four great songs during the 2019 *Country Music Association Awards*, so I started learning those songs: "Homecoming Queen" by Kelsea Ballerini, "Graveyard" by Halsey, "We Were" by Keith Urban, and "One Man Band" by Old Dominion.

I warm up quicker if I play a fast or difficult song first. For instance, Heart's "Crazy on You" is a perfect warm-up song because it contains fast strumming, quick chord changes, and the insidious F chord. The song requires a quick transition from

Am to F, and I'm more confident about tackling additional songs after I play this one. It really gets my blood pumping.

I keep a setlist of all the songs I've attempted to play. On some songs I only play the intro or the chorus. My idea is to play a 25-song mashup of choruses for my friends on my birthday. I'd like to play the mashup without stopping. However, I can't remember all the lyrics, I don't want to stop to shuffle paper, and I would need to keep moving the capo around to match my voice.

As of today, my setlist includes the following:

- Crazy on You
- Your Song
- Magic
- Paradise
- Clocks
- Talkin' Bout A Revolution
- The Wild One, Forever
- Into the Mystic
- Babe I'm Gonna Leave You
- Over the Hills and Far Away
- Tangerine
- Listen to Your Heart
- Have a Little Faith in Me
- China Grove
- Amie
- Don't Think Twice It's Alright
- Hey Hey My My
- Take It Easy
- Everybody Wants to Rule the World
- Song for Another Time
- One Step Up

In addition to the first three songs I learned that I previously mentioned, here's a list in chronological order (past to current) of the songs I've attempted to play. I'd like to be able to include a few lyrics in some of the song descriptions that follow, but I can't due to copyright issues. I could contact music publishers to try to get permission but that could take years, assuming that I would get permission in the first place.

Adam Levine - Lost Stars: Like I mentioned before, the first chord transition I was able to play was Fmaj7 to C. These are the first two chords of this song but then it transitions to G, which I could not do at that time. It was frustrating when I began and I wondered if I would ever be able to play G. This is a beautiful song and I believe it's better than anything Adam Levine has done with Maroon Five. I also like Keira Knightley's version in the film.

Poison - Every Rose Has Its Thorn: This is a classic feel-good song from the 1980s and another example of a rock band who hit it big with a ballad. This is another song from the 1980s that used Cadd9 to G. I found a strumming pattern online that worked. This is one of the easier songs to play and I enjoy singing it. The chorus is one of the best ever written.

Bob Dylan - Knockin' on Heaven's Door: I had to learn this because it brings back great memories of my family spending a day on the river and then going to the store for ice cream afterward. I also wanted to learn the song because I was almost 60 years old at the time and started thinking about my own mortality. It's a meaningful song for a senior citizen to play.

Pink Floyd - Wish You Were Here: One day I was showing my instructor the iconic intro. He told me it was incomplete and showed me the correct version, which was a bit more sophisticated. I felt silly but I didn't see any reason to try to relearn it because I was already on to other songs. Some guitarists want to play covers note-for-note but I don't care about that. I'm happy as long as I can play a song that sounds reasonably similar.

David Bowie and Queen - Under Pressure: I've always loved

this song, especially the snapping fingers at the beginning and the end. There have been so many covers of this song, but no one could sing it like David Bowie and Freddie Mercury. I pluck the intro and strum the verses. It sounds gorgeous.

The Church - Under the Milky Way: Along with "We Just Disagree," this song has the prettiest 12-string intro I've heard. I practiced it for a year and was able to get it. The challenge was trying to simulate the sound of a 12-string, so I play it with a capo on the fifth fret. However, by doing this, I discovered that I could not practice it for a sustained period of time because my fingertips would get sore. I know they shouldn't because I have calluses, but I think I was pressing down too hard without realizing it because I was trying to squeeze my fingers in the sixth and seventh frets. (For those who don't play guitar, the frets get narrower as you move up the fretboard).

I strummed the song but then I heard The Church's acoustic version. It was moving, better than the original. I couldn't find tabs or chords for it online so I asked my instructor if I could pay him to write out the tab for me. He was a music major in college, taught music classes for years, played 10 instruments, and has a great ear. Sure enough, he was able to tab it out. It gives me chills when I play it. Some people believe The Church was a one-hit wonder, and this was the song. But what a song it is, one of the greatest of all time. And I can play it, how cool is that? However, I really can't sing it very well. Given that I can play it but can't sing it, I'm still batting .500. I'll take it.

The Police - Roxanne: Sting sang a solo version of this song along with "Message in a Bottle" in the film *The Secret Policeman's Other Ball*. I can still picture him wearing army fatigues in the film. His voice was like an angel; he could really go high then. I was a young man when I watched it. It impressed me so much I went back to the theater three days in a row to see it again and again. I play different versions of this song using different techniques like picking, strumming, palm muting, and palm slapping to add percussive effects.

MGMT - Time to Pretend: I stated earlier in this book that I first heard this song at the beginning of the film *21*. I couldn't get it out of my head. I swapped out MGMT's lyrics and inserted my own. The intro to the song is so simple yet so recognizable.

The Naked and Famous - Youngblood: I first heard this song in a film several years ago. I could think of little else until I found out the name and artist. This song best matches my voice with the capo on six. Along with "Everybody Wants to Rule the World," it has some of my favorite lyrics. It's a song about the "in-between," the period of time when people are between significant relationships.

Leonard Cohen - Hallelujah: This is one of the most popular songs guitar players want to learn. I play this immediately before or after Youngblood because the capo stays on six (once I place a capo on a fret, I like to play all the songs that have the capo in that position because I don't want to take the time to stop to move the capo around). I learned this song because it's one of my wife's favorites and it's also easy to play.

Led Zeppelin - Over the Hills and Far Away: I learned this song from Shut Up and Play on YouTube.[2] The guy is one of the best teachers, although he goes a little too quickly for me sometimes. But that's fine because it's impossible for instructors to please everybody, since everyone is at a different point in their development. There are many comments underneath tutorials complaining that instructors are teaching too slow or too fast.

The production is second to none. The instructor wears a black shirt and uses a black background so all you see are his hands and the fretboard. It's very effective. It took me a month to learn the chords and notes, and a year to learn the song and play it competently. This song exposed me to hammer-ons, although I don't play it that often because I don't want to get a repetitive stress injury. I love to play it and it thrills me that I can play a Led Zeppelin song. I feel like a real guitarist when I play it because there's a lot going on and my hand is flying around the fretboard. The rhythm of the song is tricky; it's not just a simple strumming pattern. It involves picking, strumming, and playing with dynamics, all while keeping a certain rhythm. Along with "Good Riddance" and "Listen to Your Heart," I have spent more time on this song than any other. There's something about investing my time and energy in a song that makes it worthwhile when I can play it.

Neil Young - After the Gold Rush: This is my favorite Neil Young song, a beautiful ballad from 50 years ago. The lyrics were prescient and ring true today. I like to sing it because it forces me to practice my falsetto to try to match Young's high-pitched voice. However, I can't project my falsetto. Is there a physiological explanation for this? Why is it so difficult to project a falsetto? Why can some people do it while others cannot?

Led Zeppelin - Babe I'm Gonna Leave You: This is my favorite rock song of all time. The intro, the acoustic solo in the middle, and the outro are extraordinary. This is what a great song is all about: It begins with a beautiful acoustic intro, transitions to a rocker, back to acoustic, incorporates blues, and ends with the acoustic. Robert Plant said he had a cold the day they recorded this song and he wasn't happy with his singing, which is interesting because he sounds fantastic, especially when he calls his "babe" (listen to the song and you'll know what I mean).

Third Eye Blind - Jumper: Their first two albums were extraordinary. I only play the chorus. Jim Carey played it in the film *Yes Man*. This song has a great solo by Kevin Cadogan. I can't say enough about this band. They're still making great music twenty years later. Just listen to "Take A Side" or "Ways" from their 2019 release *Screamer*.

Better Than Ezra - A Lifetime: Great lyrics, great rhythm, great drumming, great song by an underrated band. It took a long time to be able to transition from Fmaj7 to C to G fast enough because the song plays at 160 bpm. One of the hallmarks of a great song is whether or not I can remember the lyrics after not hearing the song for years. This is the type of song where I want to scream the chorus at the top of my lungs while I drive to the beach in Southern California.

Brad Paisley - Last Time for Everything: It starts with a hot lick, picking muted notes in G and Em. It amazes me when I see Paisley do this so effortlessly, without looking. But that's where woodshedding will get you. It's a nostalgic song about growing old and I can identify with the message that there is a "last time for everything." Paisley can really play. Same for Keith Urban. Paisley once described Urban's talent by stating, "I think he has more natural ability than anyone I have ever met."[4] Both write great songs.

Len - Steal My Sunshine: Most people would probably be surprised that a senior citizen would play this song, given it was a favorite of the younger generation. The lyrics and the melody are extremely catchy. It's amazing how three words in a chorus can embed themselves so deep in my brain. The AEB chord progression sounds hot. However, I still can't play it correctly because I cannot form a traditional B chord, so instead I put my index finger on the A string in the second fret and my third and fourth fingers on the D and G strings in the fourth fret. It works.

Eric Church - Mr. Misunderstood: This is a great country album with memorable lyrics. It starts with a great fingerstyle lick followed by strumming. I like songs that do this because strumming sounds more explosive after fingerstyle and the styles play off of each other. It's effective when it's combined with dynamics and muting.

Eric Church - Record Year: Church is a master with lyrics and this song is a prime example. I saw him play it during a televised performance at Red Rocks. I spent a long time practicing this one. I found a strumming pattern and tried to replicate it, but it was too long and the whole process got convoluted, so I quit playing it. This is another song I need to get back to now that I can listen to a song and figure out the strumming pattern.

Coldplay - Fix You: Chris Martin has a knack for combining melodies, his voice, and chord progressions to create emotional songs that connect with the public. Their songs are ethereal and transport me to another world.

Bonnie Raitt - I Can't Make You Love Me: This is a beautiful song that pulls at the heartstrings. We've all been in relationships where we love someone but they don't love us back. We try and try but no matter what we do, we can't make them love us. Raitt is truly a great singer.

James Bay - Let It Go: This was a hit song in 2014. I only play the chorus, which is simple and beautiful. It's one of the few songs I can sing adequately. Capo on four.

Bruce Springsteen - One Step Up: This was the first Springsteen song I learned. It's a great song to practice picking. The lyrics are masterful; Springsteen has a way of describing Americana in all of its pain and glory. The song tells a story of a marriage that isn't working. How many of us can relate to the phrase, "One step up and two steps back?" Life seems to present us with the same lessons over and over until we learn them.

Brett Eldredge - Drunk on Your Love: I chose this song because it has a nice rhythm and a catchy chorus. Like many country songs, the chords are simple and it's easy to play.

Bill Withers - Ain't No Sunshine: As I write this, Bill Withers died today. With the combination of his death and COVID-19, there Ain't No Sunshine, indeed. I used to play this on the jukebox at a burger joint when I was a kid. I counted how many times he sang the two words in the chorus (26?). This is an easy song to play and one of the first songs I learned where I didn't have to strum all the time, just a few strums here and there is all it took. It's nice to add a little palm slap to give it a percussive effect during the chorus. Has there ever been a better first line in any song than this one?

Better Than Ezra - Desperately Wanting: This song has fantastic lyrics, the use of space, a hot drumbeat, and a great-sounding progression (F, hammer-on Am, G). When I started to learn it, I could not form an F chord and I also couldn't transfer from Am to G quickly enough because my skills weren't there yet. This song has a wonderful rhythm to it because after one downstroke on F, the vocals commence, followed by a quick hammer-on on Am at the end of the first line, followed by G. It sounds big. I play the version on YouTube that the band played at a radio station.[3] I watched it several times to figure out the strumming pattern. I was impressed by how easily the lead singer could play F. Of course, he has huge hands like almost every professional guitar player.

Tears for Fears - Everybody Wants to Rule the World: This is one of my favorite songs from the 1980s. It features a driving bass and it includes some of my favorite lyrics of all time. Earlier in the book I mentioned a young woman who played an acoustic cover. (She also plays an excellent cover of The Cranberries' "Linger," a song I also play). I was able to learn a technique from watching her that helps me play my version. How cool is that? That's the nature of playing a musical instrument in the age of YouTube. The three lines in the third verse give me chills and are my favorite lines in any song, with the possible exception of an iconic three-word phrase from The Who's "Baba O'Riley," easily one of the most famous lines in rock 'n roll history, primarily because it encapsulates the excesses of the 1960s. I can't include the line here due to copyright issues, but if you're a rock 'n roll fan from that era, you already know what it is.

Tom Petty and the Heartbreakers - The Wild One, Forever:

This is one of my favorite ballads and my favorite Tom Petty song. As a songwriter, Petty was at the top along with Springsteen and others. In Petty's biography, author Warren Zanes described the day Petty got his first big royalty check for $7,000 and promptly spent it all on a Camaro. Petty picked up Springsteen at the Sunset Marquis in Hollywood, after which they bought a half-dozen 8-track tapes at Tower Records. Then they drove around until they had listened to every song on every tape. At one point while listening to the Rolling Stones song "Congratulations," Springsteen raised his arms up to the sky and said, "You can take me now!"[4] What I would give to have been on that ride!

This is a beautiful song with fantastic lyrics. I like the continual picking riff throughout the song. Petty must have had an affinity for the D chord because he used it a lot. It's one of the easiest chords for me to strum because I don't have to hit the top two strings. I don't know why that is easier for me, but it is. I played this song and "Free Fallin" in his honor the day he died. It was emotional.

Maren Morris - In the Middle: I only play the chorus (Cadd9, G, D). It's fun to play because it involves quite a bit of palm muting. It's catchy and sometimes I find myself playing it for a few minutes over and over, putting me into a trance-like state. This is one of the aspects of guitar that is so seducing, getting lost in a meditational state where I'm unaware of my surroundings. I feel like I'm one with my instrument and I'm in perfect harmony with the planet. I know it's exactly what I'm supposed to be doing.

Porcupine Tree - Trains: This is one of the best songs the masses have never heard. This group has a handful of songs that are legacy-type songs. I had to learn how to play quick hammer-ons on consecutive upstrokes. Since then, I've incorporated palm muting and slapping to make it my own. I like to change songs because it feeds my creative juices and keeps me motivated. And I don't have to worry about it because I'm not playing it publicly or trying to record it for commercial purposes.

Electric Light Orchestra - Fire on High: I'll never forget the first time I heard this song. It has one of the hottest licks ever at 2:43. I can't play it perfectly because it has several fast barre chord changes, although it's been a year so maybe it's time to try again. One of my problems is that I don't play electric guitar. It's easier to play barre chords on an electric because the strings are thinner and the neck is longer so playing up around the eighth or tenth fret is not a problem compared to my acoustic, where the body meets the neck at the 12th fret. It's hard to explain but I can't get my hand at the proper angle to play barre chords in the eighth fret or higher on my acoustic.

Nevertheless, I was in the front row leaning against the stage when I saw ELO at Winterland in the late 1970s. I went crazy when they went into the hot lick in this song.

The Counting Crows - Round Here: This song has a captivating melody unlike any I heard before. I got a kick out of learning the opening lick. It was difficult for me at first because I had to barre the first and second strings in the third fret while tapping my pinky on-and-off on the fifth fret. I don't think this would be an issue for any other guitar player, but with limited mobility it was difficult for me.

In 2007, Major League Baseball gave my publisher and I VIP tickets to the All-Star game and related festivities in San Francisco. They were interested in talking to my publisher about how to leverage our companies to maximize exposure for my *Fantasy Baseball and Mathematics* books for teachers and students. I went to a pre-game party (it might have been the day before the game, I can't remember) on the wharf. It was a gorgeous day when suddenly I heard the Counting Crows. I turned around and there they were, on a stage that had been empty. I didn't know they were going to be there. It was a treat for me to see them up close. This is such an underrated band. Seeing them play at a small venue reminded me of the time when I saw The Doobie Brothers also play on the wharf in San Francisco.

Phil Collins - In the Air Tonight: I first heard this album when I was living in my college town in the early 1980s. I knew it was going to be a hit as soon as I heard the echo drums. I play it slow to increase the dramatic effect. In fact, I place a roll of pennies on the D note on my keyboard. It gives the song an eerie background sound similar to the original. And that, ladies and gentlemen, is the extent of the special effects I use when I play.

YES - Roundabout: Like I mentioned earlier, I saw YES at the Spectrum in Philadelphia in 1975. At that point, they were one of the most popular bands in the world. I'll never forget the crowd reaction when they began playing "Yours Is No Disgrace" and "Long Distance Runaround." This is an iconic song and no one can sing it like Jon Anderson. The intro (which is all I play) is one of the most famous of all time. I surprised myself when I was able to play it fingerstyle. It sounds just like the original. Thank you, Mr. Howe.

Justin Bieber - Sorry: You may be surprised that I learned a Justin Bieber song. Like I said earlier in the book, I watched a guy on YouTube incorporate percussive effects, and I wanted to try to simulate that. Like most of the songs I play, I vary the speed and the dynamics to try to make it my own. I alternate between picking and strumming in this song. The short solo took me a long time to learn before I could do it competently.

Led Zeppelin - What Is and What Should Never Be: Page's lick during the outro is the hottest I've ever heard and might be my favorite segment of any rock song. Nobody could use space like Page could. When you combine that with Robert Plant's primal screams and rapping (which is essentially what he was doing) you get quintessential Zeppelin, way ahead of their time.

Dobie Gray - Drift Away: I started playing this with a friend. There's never been a better chorus in any other song, with perhaps the single greatest line of any song. It's simply one of the greatest songs ever written. It's fun to play and takes me back to high school.

Dave Mason - We Just Disagree: Since I don't have a 12-string, I play this in Open E because it sounds big. Playing in Open E forced me to use some different fingerings compared to those I use in standard tuning. I also enjoyed learning the short intro because it's a technique I hadn't done before, yet another tool in my arsenal. I've learned something from almost every song I've learned how to play, whether it's a bend here, a two-finger hammer-on there, a slide here, or a little vibrato there. I tried playing this song in standard tuning but it doesn't sound nearly as hot.

Roxette - Listen to Your Heart: One day I was at a music store when one of the owners played the first minute of this song fingerstyle. I asked if he was willing to give me a lesson on it. I videotaped him playing it, then came home and rewound it a few dozen times to learn the first minute of the song. I've been playing it a few times a week for over a year but I still can't play it perfectly, although I'm getting there. This song has improved my fingerstyle abilities considerably. There's a few hammer-ons, bends, and slides, and I'd never used those techniques in conjunction with fingerstyle. I like to strum the first verse and then transition to fingerstyle. It gives an edge to the song and makes it sound as though I'm better than I really am. The guy who taught it to me learned it from a gentleman on YouTube named Igor Presnyakov.

James Taylor - Fire and Rain: I started playing this with a friend. This is a classic song from one of the best singer-songwriters who ever lived. I never get tired of playing this one and the chorus includes the typical JT lyrics that stick with you. I still can't figure out exactly what he's doing with the A chord at the end of the chorus, but that's just a minor technicality. When I first started to play guitar, I wanted to play the songs note-for-note just like the originals, but after awhile, who really cares?

John Hiatt - Have a Little Faith in Me: This might be my favorite pop song. With all due respect to Donny Hathaway, this is the best male vocal I've ever heard. It was difficult for me to learn because there are a lot of F chords and I have only recently been able to play that chord.

Led Zeppelin - Tangerine: This song is exotic and beautiful. The descending baseline reminds me of the Beatles' "While My Guitar Gently Weeps." It took me awhile to learn it but I have it down. How brilliant was Jimmy Page to create something like this? If you don't know by now, he was pretty good.

Led Zeppelin - The Rain Song: I don't play this one often because it's the only song I play in its tuning (DGCGCD) and I don't like to take the time to retune. Once I start playing, I don't like to stop. I only learned the beginning of this song but it's stunning. I can't think of a more beautiful song by any rock 'n roll band in the last 50 years.

Peter, Paul and Mary - Don't Think Twice, It's All Right: This is a song a friend turned me onto. I struggled with it initially because some parts of it are fast and it includes a quick transition to F. I have it now, but it took a lot of practice. It's also a song I enjoy singing. This is an example of a song that, prior to playing it, I would not have chosen to learn. It was just another song. But songs have a tendency to grow on us, and this is one that I now enjoy.

Eagles - Peaceful Easy Feeling: Similar to the prior song, this is another tune that I would not have chosen to play if not for a friend's recommendation. However, I now love to play this song. It's easy to play and has a wonderful laid-back vibe to it. You can't go wrong playing Eagles' songs.

James Taylor - Sweet Baby James: This is another classic song. Taylor's ability to create lyrics (especially choruses) that stick in the subconscious mind is unsurpassed. This song gives me the opportunity to practice F#m, a difficult chord for me.

America - Ventura Highway: The intro lick takes a lot of practice with some quick changes that involve muting. It's tricky and I still haven't mastered it. I play various parts of the song but have yet to put the complete song together. There's only so much time. But the opening lick to this song is one of my favorites, it's so rhythmic. America wrote some of the greatest songs, and their catalog includes plenty of classics. I don't know if there's any other song that takes me back to the early 1970s like "A Horse with No Name."

Old Dominion - Written In the Sand: I believe this band currently writes some of the best lyrics in music today. Their songs are catchy and easy to sing along to. I particularly enjoyed watching them on *Songland*.

Chris Lane - Take Back Home Girl: Songs like this puzzle me when they don't go to the top of the charts. This is a great song, a perfect song for a road trip. The chorus is a monster. The main riff starts with a couple of quick consecutive hammer-ons on the A and D strings. That was something new for me at the time.

Montrose - Rock Candy; Make It Last: I was such a huge Montrose fan in high school that during the graduation ceremony I used his name in place of my real middle name. The card reader called it as such and the gymnasium exploded in cheers. Well, maybe not so much. It was a silly adolescent gesture but it made me happy at the time.

These two songs were on Montrose's debut album, which sold four million copies.[15] The story goes that Sammy Hager went to Montrose's house to play four songs for him that he had written: "Make It Last," "Bad Motor Scooter," "I Don't Want It," and "One Thing on My Mind." Then Montrose played "Rock the Nation." Hager had the lyrics to "Space Station #5" so Montrose came up with the riff.[39] What a day of absolute insane creativity!

I play the main riffs from these two songs on my acoustic, so it sounds nothing like the heavy sound that Montrose got out of his Les Paul. Unfortunately, Ronnie Montrose died of cancer in 2012, a sad day.

The Doobie Brothers - China Grove: This is one of the songs I listened to the most in high school. A cover band named Open Road played this song and "Long Train Runnin" at local dances. I was known to dance across the stage while they played these songs. I must've looked like an idiot but I guess I was too young and naive to realize it. I've been playing this song several times a week for six months. There are some quick changes with chords that I'm not used to (C#m to F#m to C#m, F to Fsus4 to F, B to E (power chord) to B.

Blue Oyster Cult - Don't Fear the Reaper: I couldn't call myself a rocker if I didn't learn the classic riff that opens this song. The key is letting the last note ring at the end of each of the four chords. This song reminds me of an old friend who completely lost it when he heard the song at lunchtime during high school.

Mazzy Star - Fade Into You: The lead singer has an ethereal voice, very unique. I only play the chorus. There's something about the dream pop/neo-psychedelia sound that touches me. It's a magical sound that takes me to another world.

Bruce Springsteen - She's the One: I get a kick out of playing Springsteen songs because I imagine I'm Springsteen. Now all I have to do is play gigs for decades, get one of the best bands in the world to back me up, sell millions of records, develop one of the most authentic, gritty voices in rock 'n roll, and write the best rock 'n roll songs the world has ever heard, and I'll be right there with him.

The Cranberries - Linger: I've loved this song ever since it came out 30 years ago. Rest in peace Dolores (the former lead singer). She had such a distinctive voice, truly one of a kind. They have an acoustic version I like better than the original. The strings make this song, especially when they come in during the intro. Similar to The Cure, The Cranberries take me back to the 1990s. There's nothing wrong with a little nostalgia and sentimentality, especially for someone on the back nine of life.

The Cranberries - Why: This is a gorgeous song I found in 2019. It made me wonder, how many great songs are there that I'm not aware of? This song is easy to play, a fun one to sing, and has a great strumming pattern. I play their acoustic version, which begins with a beautiful acoustic intro.

The Pure Prairie League - Amie: This is another song I would've never chosen to play if not for the recommendation from a friend. Now it's one of my favorites to play. It has a great rhythm, and of all the songs I play it's the one song that forces me to keep my strumming hand moving all the time. This is important because I've developed a bad habit of stopping my strumming hand. But there's no time to stop during this song.

One day when I played this song, I suddenly broke into "Crazy on You." There was a point in the song (an Esus4/B chord) that was a natural transition for the mashup. I didn't think about it beforehand, it just happened, which is one of the great things about playing guitar - the creativity and unlimited possibilities to play songs within songs, or adding my own flavor to the song by switching chords around, changing accents on strumming patterns, or playing the song faster or slower, softer or louder, or in a different key. When I play, I feel as though the world is my oyster and I'm in charge. The creativity feeds my soul.

Interestingly, I was raised in a family where creativity was not encouraged. When I was a young boy, we had a piano and my mom would play it once in awhile, but that was the extent of the creativity in our house. Thus, I grew up believing I wasn't creative because I did not know how to paint, draw, dance, sing, or any other creative endeavor. However, when I started teaching, I found I had a penchant for creating engaging lessons that could motivate students to learn, and I developed some of those lessons into books. I believe everyone is creative; the key is finding the context or medium that gives us an opportunity to express that creativity.

Neil Young - Hey Hey My My: I use my falsetto to sing this one. I can't project it so I sing it softly. This song has one of the most classic riffs ever created. And it's simple to do. I'd like to learn how to play harmonica so I could add that component like Young does. In his autobiography, he goes into detail about the equipment he uses. I forgot what amps and pedals he uses on this song, but it's the best sounding acoustic guitar I've ever heard. It's rich and huge.

Neil Young - Heart of Gold: This was an easy song to learn in just a few minutes. I don't choose to spend a lot of time playing easy songs because I want to challenge myself to learn new songs and techniques. But I come back to this song occasionally because it reminds me of my teenage years and all the good times I had in high school.

Eagles - Lyin' Eyes: I only play the first couple of verses because it's a long song and I have a lot of songs to go through every day. The Eagles' lyrics are captivating because they create visceral stories. That's one of the reasons they're one of the best-selling acts of all time, along with the fact that they're great technicians at their craft. Interestingly, I was never a fan in high school, but I can't get enough of them the last few years. I recently saw one of their reunion concerts on television and *every song* was a classic. How many bands can say that?

Supertramp - Give a Little Bit: This is one of my favorite bands. It took a great deal of practice to get this song down, especially the rhythm of the progression from D to A7 to G. I purchased the sheet music because I had concerns about some chords at the end of the song, so I ended up using different chords rather than some of the chords on the sheet music. Why would I do that? Because it's more pleasing to my ear. It's a great rhythm guitar song for an acoustic. I like the ending; there's two different ways I play it and sometimes I'll play both endings. Why not? This is one of the benefits of playing by yourself because when you're playing for someone you have to stay within the confines of the song. I like to play mashups, or play certain parts of certain songs repeatedly, or skip some parts, etc. Sometimes the Guitar Gods take over and who knows what's coming next.

Lady Gaga and Bradley Cooper - Shallow: This song is from the remake of *A Star is Born*. It knocked me out when I heard it in the film. However, it's not easy for me to play and I still cannot play it at the correct tempo. One of the challenges to playing guitar is that after awhile I know so many songs, licks, and riffs that it becomes impossible to practice them on a regular basis. Like I said earlier, I rotate songs but there's no systematic way I do it and therefore I might not play a song for a year or so. It's not intentional. Out of sight, out of mind, as they say. Then when I get back to the song, I often can't remember how to play it, although it's in my brain somewhere and usually after a few minutes the song will come back in bits and pieces. But when it doesn't, I have to go back to YouTube and watch a tutorial to figure out how to do it. When that occurs, I feel like I'm not spending my time wisely, so it's important for me to stay current with all of my songs. I've invested so much time and energy to learn the songs that I don't want to forget how to play them. There are times when I'll be in the middle of a song, and suddenly I remember a song (or a portion of) that I had forgotten how to play. When that happens, I immediately begin playing that song because I don't want to forget how to play it. My rationale is there must be a reason that the song suddenly came into my head. It's as if my subconscious is presenting me with the opportunity to play the song again and I better do so right then and there or I might lose it for eternity. One of these days I'll get smart and shoot video of all the songs I've learned so I can refer to it if I forget how to play them.

Eagles - Take It Easy: I had my first guitar for only a week in 2015 when a friend came over. Although he hadn't played for some time, he picked up my guitar and launched into this song. I was completely blown away. I would give anything to be able to do that, I thought. Well, now I can and what an incredible feeling it is. It never ceases to amaze me what can emerge from the combination of an acoustic guitar and the human voice. Sometimes the tears start flowing when I play. Is there any other hobby with that kind of impact? I recently learned the intro lick, which I had been looking for, although it doesn't sound as good on an acoustic compared to an electric.

Pete Townshend - Let My Love Open the Door: I'd forgotten about this song until I heard it in 2018. It's one of the fastest songs I play in terms of switching chords. When I first started learning barre chords, I shied away from them because they were difficult and I couldn't play them at all. But now I use them all the time because that's the only way I'm going to get proficient with them. There's a young lady who plays a cover of this on YouTube.[5] Her version is gorgeous and it demonstrates how a good voice can carry a song.

Tommy James and the Shondells - Crystal Blue Persuasion: This is one of my favorite songs from my youth. My other favorite by this band is "Crimson and Clover," but it's impossible to replicate the echo on that song so I chose this one. I learned a new technique in this song, muting the E and A strings in the second fret while tapping my pinky on-and-off on the D string in the fourth fret. It's quite a stretch for my fingers. One amazing thing about guitar is how many different techniques there are.

Elton John - Your Song: Earlier, I wrote about this song and the role it played (or rather, didn't) in my marriage proposal. Initially, it was too difficult for me to play, but a few months later I came back to it and I've been working on it almost daily. It's a challenge for me to transition to Em7 because I have to roll my wrist a little bit before I can do it, and that little fraction of a second makes it difficult to maintain tempo. I'm doing this throughout the song with a couple of other chords as well, so this song is a tough one for me. When I drink green tea, this is usually the first song I play to take advantage of the caffeine. The other songs I like to take advantage of include "China Grove," "Sweet Baby James," "Don't Think Twice It's All Right," and "Crazy on You."

Interestingly, John described his songwriting process in his autobiography. Bernie Taupin wrote lyrics at night and John would find the lyrics on his piano in the morning. He would then set chords to the lyrics. One day he wrote three songs before lunchtime, including "Rocket Man."[6] Talk about prolific, that's the definition of it right there.

Heart - Crazy on You: As I stated earlier, this is the ultimate warm-up song for me because of fast strumming and a quick transition from Am to F. It also contains a nice sounding progression: F#m/D/C#m/D. I'll never forget purchasing *Dreamboat Annie* when I was in high school. It was the first time I ever thought of women as rock 'n roll idols.

I read Ann and Nancy Wilson's book last year. It was one of the best books I've read because it came from a female perspective. I thought Nancy Wilson was the hottest woman in the world when I was in high school, a female rock 'n roll guitar player.

Beatles - When I'm Sixty-Four: I will be 64 later this year so this seemed like an appropriate song to learn. There are a couple of tricky parts in this song, one of which includes transitioning quickly from F to Fm to C/G to A to D7 to G7 to C. I can play this progression in tempo if I practice it in isolation and do it over and over again, but I struggle with it when I play the song. It's more difficult playing a progression in a song because it jumps up on me, versus practicing it in isolation where I can get into a rhythm.

Glen Campbell - Wichita Lineman: This is a riveting song written by Jimmy Webb. It takes me back to my grandma's house when I was a kid because she had the album. I play it slow to make it more dramatic. It has a very short solo, one of the first solos I learned. It also has some mesmerizing lyrics, including two of the greatest lines any songwriter has created, the fourth and fifth lines in the second verse. Glen Campbell was an amazing musician and guitar player. It's a shame the younger generation of guitar players don't listen to his songs, unless they hear them in movies or television shows. After all, it's not like there are a lot of 20-year-old shredders who play Glen Campbell songs. But they could learn a thing or two from this guy, or Chet Atkins, or Roy Clark, or numerous other country guitarists. Those guys could play anything.

Van Morrison - I'll Be Your Lover Too: This is the song I can sing the best. I found my voice when I started singing it because I discovered a Joplin-like growl deep in me somewhere. If somebody asked me to play three songs, this would be one of them.

The Guess Who - No Time: This is one of the most underrated songs and bands of all time. The rhythm and melody of the outro is absolutely magnetic. It's impossible for me not to sing it when I hear it.

Which brings up a question: If you wrote a song and had only enough material for either a great intro or a great outro, which would you choose? I vote for the outro because that's what leaves a lasting impression. There are many songs that start off slowly, only to get better and better. Conversely, there are songs that have a great intro but the magic isn't there once they hit the verse. A perfect song would have it all: a great intro, verses, pre-chorus, chorus, bridge, and outro. But how many songs are like that? Off the top of your head, can you think of any songs where you love every part of the song? Or do you find yourself waiting for your favorite parts?

Ten Years After - I'd Love to Change the World: Alvin Lee's guitar talks to me. It has an incredible tone and like I stated earlier, this solo is one of the greatest of all time. Indeed, it's probably my favorite solo. The lyrics remain as true today as they did when it was first released. I recently learned the riff that underscores the song. I was excited when I began learning it. I would've never thought it was possible before I started playing guitar. Why didn't I start playing guitar earlier? I ask myself that question all the time. Anybody can do it, it just takes practice.

Sam Hunt - Kinfolks: I immediately had to learn the picking riff once I heard this song. It turns out the chords are simple but it's the muting and picking pattern that give it the flavor: A muted F chord (strings 5432), un-muted F, Am, G (strings 6432), Am, G. It sounds hot. I like to mute off-and-on because it sounds more pleasing to my ear.

Bob Seger - Night Moves: I saw them play this at Winterland in San Francisco after it was released in 1976. I liked it the first time I heard it. The opening riff is simple, yet so effective. It's one of the most memorable in rock 'n roll history. This is truly a classic song by one of the greatest singer-songwriters. And the lyrics? Among the best ever.

Lindsey Buckingham - Trouble: This is such an emotional song when Lindsey sings it. It's powerful with a great hook. It took me awhile to learn the basic riff and then I found out he actually plays it in an alternative tuning. It's a great song to practice fingerstyle. Buckingham is such an underrated guitar player.

Keith Urban - We Were: I saw this on the 2019 CMA's. He did an acoustic performance and the song touched me. He alternates between strumming and picking. I like the story about being young and in love, and later on in life reflecting back and realizing that for a short period of time he and his girlfriend "were." I've been working on picking without looking but I'm not there yet. I'd also like to learn Urban's solo from "Stupid Boy."

Bachman-Turner Overdrive - Let It Ride: I play a simple version with open chords. What a great opening riff, one of the classics from the 1970s. I used to play air guitar on this song during parties in high school. I couldn't get enough of the main riff right after the bridge. It's one of the most iconic riffs ever created. Bachman's strumming pattern used space brilliantly. This is easily one of the most recognizable rock songs ever written. The song's title stemmed from an incident where a couple of trucks boxed in the BTO tour bus on a highway. When they stopped at a rest area, band members confronted the truckers, who told them to "let it ride."[7]

Kelsea Ballerini - Homecoming Queen: I heard her play this song during the 2019 CMA's. She played on a small stage in the middle of the audience, just her and her guitar. Talk about pressure! I don't understand why bands don't do more of this sort of thing. I've been to many concerts and only once did a band ever go out to a smaller stage in the audience to do an acoustic set. Surprisingly, The Rolling Stones did this when I saw them in the 1990s. It was the highlight of the night because it was raw and intimate. (Incidentally, this was the only concert where I didn't have to buy tickets because a parent of two of my students gave me tickets). This is another fingerstyle song; I need to play more of them because I become a better guitar player when I use that style.

Halsey - Graveyard: This is another song I heard on the CMA's. Halsey joined Lady Antebellum to sing one of their songs and then they rolled into this one. Halsey's voice dances around the lyrics with all of her pitch changes. She has lived a hard life; at one point she was homeless living on the streets in New York City and considered suicide.[8] Now look where she is. The lyrics in this song are deep. Truly, it's difficult to imagine loving someone more profoundly than the lyrics portray in this song.

Taylor Swift - Miss Americana and the Heartbreak Prince: Like I stated earlier, I learned the piano riff to this song. It didn't take me long and it made me consider allocating some of the time I spend playing guitar for keyboards. Would that make me a better-rounded artist? I think it would. Then why don't I do it? I don't know.

Bruce Springsteen - Dancing in the Dark: This song has a great hard-driving rhythm and is classic E Street Band at their best. The lyrics are memorable. It continually amazes me how an artist like Springsteen can write so many great lyrics for so many great songs. I would think the "well would be dry," after an artist writes hundreds of songs. I guess there is a lot to say.

Train - Hey Soul Sister: This song contains a couple of my favorite lines. I play this with the capo on the fourth fret to simulate the sound of a ukulele. I believe this and "Drops of Jupiter" are Train's best songs. Let's face it, the piano intro in "Drops of Jupiter" is one of the all-time greats. It's so simple, yet so melodic, it brings you right in.

Old Dominion - Song for Another Time: What a clever song! It uses titles and well-known lyrics from choruses of several hit songs to tell a story. It's brilliant and I enjoy trying to guess the songs they pulled from to use in this song. I can't say enough about this band. I liked every song on their debut album, which was unusual for me.

Old Dominion - One Man Band: This song begins with an arpeggiated picking pattern that sounds beautiful. Throw in great lyrics and you have a monster hit on your hands. This is the first song I played that incorporated hybrid picking. The chorus sticks with me for a long time. Even if I play the song only one time, I find myself singing it in my mind for the rest of the day.

Led Zeppelin - Kashmir: This is one of my favorite songs to

play. It's all I played for three days once I learned it. There's something hypnotic about it and I get lost when I play it. Many Zeppelin fans consider this their favorite track. Thank you, Jimmy.

The Cure - Friday I'm in Love: There's nothing like Gothic rock to make me feel nostalgic. I was in San Jose at a minor-league baseball game at some point during the 1980s when I heard The Cure playing. I left the game and walked over to the concert. It was sold out so I sat down and listened for awhile. There's something about this type of music that makes me nostalgic, happy, and sad. I can't explain it but then again, isn't that the beauty of music? It cannot be put into words, but that doesn't mean I won't try.

Van Morrison - Into the Mystic: I first heard this when I saw the film *Immediate Family* in 1989. At that time, I thought it was a nice song but that was the extent of it. However, the song has grown on me during my senior years. It's simple to play, especially the lick that gives it the flavor. Plus it's fun to sing.

Uriah Heap - The Wizard: This has to be one of the greatest songs the masses have never heard. The melody is infectious. I enjoy playing it with different strumming patterns. Uriah Heap is at the top of the list of underrated bands.

One Republic - Apologize; The Script - Breakeven; A Great Big World - Say Something: I'm lumping these three together because they have three of the most amazing choruses I've heard. Whoever wrote these songs is brilliant. Choruses don't get more powerful than these. The capo stays on the third fret for all three songs so I play them consecutively.

Aerosmith - Sweet Emotion: Has there ever been a hotter intro in any rock song than the bass riff in this one? I don't think so. Thank you, Mr. Hamilton. This is an iconic song for anyone who grew up listening to rock 'n roll in the 1970s. Tyler's voice and lyrics provide the sass, and Joe Perry used a talk box on this one. In my book, Joe Perry is right there in the top tier of guitar players. Not because of solos, but because he has the unique ability (like Keith Richards, the master) to create riffs that make us want to move.

Coldplay - Clocks; Paradise; and Magic: I learned the riffs to these songs in one day. I was excited because they are three of my favorite Coldplay songs and they are simple to play.

Katy Perry - Daisies. Like I stated earlier, I learned this from Katy Perry's guitar lesson on YouTube. It's only three chords, all muted: G, Bm, A. The chord progression is fast and it's difficult for me to transition from G to Bm in tempo with the capo on the third fret. I need to contort my body and that takes an extra split-second so I need to practice it more.

There are plenty of additional songs I've played around with, but these are the songs I've put the most time into. I keep telling myself I've learned enough songs and I need to focus on mastering them. But then I hear songs I want to play (I'm currently learning Bad Company's "Feel Like Makin' Love"), so my setlist keeps getting longer. Even if I could play 1,000 songs, I would still want to learn new songs. It's human nature to want to grow and learn. This is why guitar players are hunter-gatherers when it comes to songs. For those who choose, playing guitar can guarantee a lifetime of professional development on the instrument.

CHAPTER ELEVEN

NO BAD DAYS

"Do what you can, with what you have, where you are."[1]
Theodore Roosevelt

IS THERE any other way to live life? I don't think so.

I do everything I can to maximize my potential. This includes attention to my diet and breathing (one of the advantages of singing), as well as reflexology, stretching, and exercise.

I do not eat any microwave food, processed food, canned food, boxed food, junk food, or added sugar. Every day, my diet includes eight glasses of water, a bowl of steel cut oats, 15 servings of raw vegetables and fruits, a small bowl of assorted baked beans, and one or two ounces of raw assorted nuts and seeds. This represents my foundation and it has served me well because I've only been sick once in 35 years.

I used to tell my students I eat well because I want to feel as good I can, as often as I can. This includes eating foods that are rich in tyrosine, the amino acid necessary for dopamine production. Foods high in tyrosine include cheese, almonds, walnuts, seeds, oatmeal, fish, eggs, meat, fruits, seaweed, yogurt, green tea, velvet beans, and green vegetables. Lifestyle choices also play a role in dopamine levels, including getting enough sleep, exercise, and sunlight. Listening to music has also been found to increase the release of dopamine. If you eat these foods and follow this lifestyle, you will be healthier and feel better.

None other than Hippocrates stated, "Let food be thy medicine, and medicine be thy food."[2] Many people do not eat what is considered food. They eat candy, snacks, and junk, which is not really food, given the complete lack of nutrients. Our bodies are not made to break down these substances. In the long-term, they cause problems. I think of my body as a fine-tuned machine, and the only fuel I use is premium quality food. If you're eating the standard American diet (SAD) then you're not going to maximize your potential on the guitar, or in life for that matter. "Garbage in, garbage out," as they say. Or, "You are what you eat." The reason phrases like this withstand the test of time is because there's credibility to them, some semblance of truth.

I start my day with 16 oz. of warm water. This keeps me "regular" and helps to flush out toxins. Thirty minutes later I eat a bowl of steel cut oatmeal (presoaked for 24 hours) along with half an avocado, a banana, and a hard-boiled egg. Lunch is usually beans or tofu with vegetables and wonder noodles. My afternoon snack is usually organic blueberries with raw nuts and seeds. Dinner is a huge salad with a combination of 10 fruits and vegetables and an olive, onion and garlic pâté my wife makes, topped with coconut aminos. My after dinner snack is usually a bowl of air-popped popcorn topped with cinnamon, sea salt, and either coconut aminos or organic cold-processed olive oil.

I sleep nine hours a night, have little stress in my life (I'm retired), and I work out an hour a day on the treadmill. In addition, I don't drink alcohol or smoke. I'm not currently on any type of medication and I am in excellent health. Perhaps this is why - even though several guitar players told me that they have good days and bad days on the guitar - all my days are about the same. I don't really have any bad days. Logic follows that if I don't have bad days, improvement will come quicker, in large part because motivation stays high. Now, I have had days where I don't seem to have it that day, but as I continue to play those days often turn out to be the best days. In other words, some days it just takes me longer to warm up. Also, I never play when I'm tired or hungry.

When I used to tell students about my diet, they told me they could not eat like me because they had to have their comfort foods: Cookies, pizza, ice cream, etc. I told them (according to ancient Eastern medicine), once the body is in balance it no longer craves sugar, sodium, or fat. It might take awhile for the body to adjust, but once it does the cravings go away.

I had bouts of brain fog several years ago. I had difficulty with short-term memory and had problems recalling words during conversations. One day I saw a doctor on television discussing his book, *Grain Brain*. The book explains the poisonous effect gluten has on the brain, which in turn poisons the body.[3] I stopped eating gluten and the brain fog disappeared. This was before I started playing guitar, but I include it here because if you are allergic or even sensitive to gluten, it could have an effect on your brain's ability to function. If your brain is not functioning properly, you are not going to be able to maximize your potential.

BEFORE I RETIRED, I occasionally walked to a nearby store to buy a smoothie. One day I was playing in an auditorium on campus while I waited for my instructor. It all seemed to be happening that day while I warmed up. I was better than I'd ever been. I couldn't believe how much I had improved in one day. It didn't make sense.

I was at the store a few weeks later waiting for my smoothie, when I discovered that my drink had a shot of green energy in it. The smoothies had given me a little buzz and I didn't realize it. This is why I was playing so well on that prior day. Given that my system was not used to caffeine, it had given my body quite a kick. My reflexes were a little bit quicker and I was able to anticipate what was coming next. I was dialed in. Suddenly, I realized why the masses are addicted to caffeine. I started experimenting with green tea because it has approximately one-third the amount of caffeine compared to a regular cup of coffee. I drank half of one cup of green tea, which is roughly one-sixth of one cup of coffee. It worked. I didn't feel a buzz because green tea has a gradual effect compared to coffee. I did this for a few days and found I was able to play better. Then one day I didn't drink it and I had a headache. It was awful. Even though I drank such a small amount of caffeine for only a few days, my system was so clean that I had withdrawal symptoms. I discovered if I skipped a day, my body did not get used to caffeine, so there were no withdrawal symptoms. I tried that and it worked for about a week, but then I got a headache again because even though the half-life of caffeine can be up to five hours, it can take quite awhile for the human body to flush out the remaining caffeine.[4] So I gave it up for a year. As of this writing, however, I have been using it again every few days without any repercussions. And I love it. How long will this last? Probably until I get my next headache. Many things in life are a trade-off, which begs the question: Am I willing to deal with a headache every once in awhile in order to get the benefits from playing with caffeine in my system? I don't know.

Compounding the situation is the fact that coffee is an acidic food. Many health professionals believe acidic foods facilitate disease, and alkaline foods promote health. The theory is that the pH of an acidic body will test below 7.5 while the pH of an alkaline body will test above 7.5.[5] Plus, let's not forget that caffeine is a drug that restricts blood flow in the brain, and can raise blood pressure as well as increase the risk of headaches, indigestion, incontinence, insomnia, depression, anxiety, and heart attacks.[6] And yet, even with this knowledge, I still want my kick when I play.

GIVEN my age and the fact that my surgeon told me I had an increased chance of getting tendinitis in my arm, I stretch every day before and after I play. I stretch my forearms and biceps and do some wrist rolls in both directions. Sometimes I stretch my fingers by gently pulling them one-by-one back toward me and holding for a few seconds, as I hold my arm out straight. This is a contrarian movement because guitarists' fingers are usually curled in toward the palm of their hand. My chiropractor thought these exercises were an excellent idea. I believe this is why I haven't had any problems with tendinitis, and I am deeply grateful for that. I know adolescents in high school who already have elbow and wrist problems from playing. This usually stems from poor posture because their guitar neck is too low and therefore they have to bend their wrists unnaturally when they play. The closer the guitar neck is to the head, the better the chance of mitigating potential problems from improper alignment.

Speaking of injuries, one day a friend sent me a video of him finger tapping on an electric. I thought it was one of the hottest licks I ever heard and I immediately contacted my instructor to see if he could figure out how to play it. He did, and so for a couple of weeks I spent 10 or 15 minutes a day practicing finger tapping. At my age and having had surgery on my fretting arm, I was concerned that I was more susceptible to repetitive stress injury, so I quit finger tapping after awhile. Priorities.

Sedentary lifestyles have significant implications for health, so it's important to keep moving. I do a number of leg, back, and abdominal stretches after I play each day because I've been sitting for two hours. I also do Kegel exercises, which supports the pelvic floor, bladder, intestines, and prostate (and uterus for women). Kegel exercises can be done anywhere, anytime, sitting or standing.

One of the most important exercises I do is reflexology, the Chinese tradition of massaging feet, ears, or hands to stimulate energy (qi) to flow throughout the body. Studies indicate reflexology may be able to significantly reduce stress and blood pressure.[7] There are 7,000 nerve endings in feet that are connected to specific points in the body. I use a massage gun (one of the greatest inventions) on the bottom of my feet, as well as other parts of my body that are sore. I find the tender spots and focus on those, especially the points that are connected to my thyroid because I was recently diagnosed hypothyroid. After further testing, my thyroid was normal, but I don't want to take any chances so I stimulate my thyroid by applying pressure to the corresponding points located on the bottom of my feet.

The thyroid has an extremely important role in the human body, and it is often misunderstood. The thyroid gland regulates body temperature and impacts metabolism, growth, and development. There is an ongoing debate as to whether soy or cruciferous vegetables can negatively impact the thyroid. Some studies indicate that soy doesn't impact the thyroid if iodine levels are normal. One study found that soy negatively impacted women but not men. Whatever the case, I believe it is prudent to get tested for thyroid function, especially if you aren't feeling well and the doctor can't find anything wrong. I've met people who struggled for years with various maladies only to finally discover the culprit was their thyroid.

The three most important things we can do for our health are exercise, get enough sleep, and maintain a nutritious diet. One benefit of intense exercise is that it allows us to breathe deeply. Deep breathing supplies our blood and cells with new oxygen and expels old carbon dioxide. Much has been written describing the benefits of deep breathing. They include reducing stress, lowering heart rate, and lowering blood pressure.[8]

Now, contrast my lifestyle with rock 'n roll bands that stayed up all night, had terrible diets, and had substance abuse problems. There were plenty of sober musicians in the 1960s and 1970s, but for those who were not sober, how good would they have been if they had chosen drug-free lifestyles? Even though many musicians have talked about the link between drugs and the creative process, the fact is we'll never know the quality of music they would have produced otherwise.

It's easy to see why so many bands relied on drugs. They often didn't get off stage until after midnight and were so amped up they couldn't sleep during the night. They tried to sleep during the day but it was difficult because they were traveling so their sleep cycle was messed up. They were tired when it was time to go on stage, so from their perspective their only option was to ingest substances to stay awake. It was a vicious cycle and it's a wonder more musicians didn't collapse on stage or cancel a show. There was a warrior-like mentality that no matter what, you got on stage and performed because you owed it to your fans.

"The show must go on" is an appropriate phrase here. I don't know why the show must go on; maybe it's the potential of disappointing fans and the subsequent blowback, or the coordination it would take to reschedule, or the absence of revenue from that show. I wonder how many band members were strung out at the concerts I saw when I was in high school. It doesn't matter though, because young fans don't care, they just want to see their favorite artists no matter what. Indeed, rational thought often goes out the window when adolescents are at rock concerts. For example, I was at an Aerosmith concert once when lead singer Steven Tyler spit into the crowd. Several fans put their hands up so they could catch it. Dream on.

CHAPTER TWELVE

REMINISCE LISTS

"Without music, life would be a mistake."[1] Friedrich Nietzsche

MY FIRST THREE albums when I was a kid were *Get Ready* by Rare Earth, *Three Dog Night Live at the Forum,* and the Beatles' *Sgt. Pepper's Lonely Hearts Club Band*. I listened to them on my parents' old stereo console until they bought me an inexpensive turntable with built-in speakers. The sound was horrible but I didn't know any better. I remember air drumming to the drum solo to "Get Ready," a 21-minute song. I had that solo down! Other tracks from these albums that stood out included "One," "Chest Fever," and "Eli's Comin'" (Three Dog Night), and "With a Little Help From My Friends" and "Lucy in the Sky With Diamonds" (Beatles). The latter song was a game changer for me because I'd never heard psychedelic music. Years later, I enjoyed listening to bands like YES, Uriah Heap, and Emerson, Lake and Palmer, who had a similar sound.

During eighth grade, I remember the Jackson Five's "ABC," B.J. Thomas' "Raindrops Keep Falling on My Head," Free's "All Right Now," Sugarloaf's "Green-Eyed Lady," Simon and

Garfunkel's "Cecilia" and "Bridge Over Troubled Water," Creedence Clearwater Revival's "Up Around the Bend," and The Kinks "Lola." I recall warming up before basketball games to "Sweet Georgia Brown," the Harlem Globetrotters theme song. Our coach tried to install a disciplined offensive scheme at practices but we thought we were the Globetrotters and it drove him crazy. I remember dancing to The Grass Roots' "Temptation Eyes" and the Carpenters' "Close to You" at eighth grade dances and not knowing what to say to a girl when the song finished. It was awkward.

The heavens parted in high school when my English class got to listen to music in class. If memory serves, we listened to the same album every day. That album was *The Best of Bread*. I had those songs memorized, and there were some classics: "If," "Make It with You," "Everything I Own," and "Baby I'm-a Want You." Listening to music in school was a foreign concept to me and a revelation. Like many adolescent males, I pushed the envelope. I asked the teacher if I could bring in my Montrose and Doobie Brothers records to play in class. I salivated at the thought of writing my essays to "Bad Motor Scooter" or "China Grove." I'll let you guess what the answer was.

I recently looked at the Billboard Year-End Hot 100 singles for my high school years (1971-1975).[2] I was stunned because I could remember the melodies in many of the 500 songs, the majority of which I hadn't heard in 45 years. Such is the power of music. The melodies were still in my subconscious somewhere, more retrievable compared to conversations or events that took place at that time, at least in my case.

At any rate, the following is a list of 10 songs from each of my high school years that are most representative of that year and immediately take me back to that point in time. If you are a music lover from my generation, chances are you can recall the melody in many of these songs.

1971

- Mr. Bojangles by Nitty Gritty Dirt Band
- It's Too Late by Carol King
- Theme from *Shaft* by Isaac Hayes
- Joy to the World by Three Dog Night
- You've Got a Friend by James Taylor
- One Less Bell to Answer by The 5th Dimension
- Ain't No Sunshine by Bill Withers
- What's Going On by Marvin Gaye
- If You Could Read My Mind by Gordon Lightfoot
- Maggie May by Rod Stewart

1972

- Anticipation by Carly Simon
- The Candy Man by Sammy Davis Jr.
- Doctor My Eyes by Jackson Browne
- American Pie by Don McLean
- Heart of Gold by Neil Young
- I Can See Clearly Now by Johnny Nash
- My Ding-a-Ling by Chuck Berry
- Go All the Way by Raspberries
- A Horse With No Name by America
- Day After Day by Badfinger

1973

- Crocodile Rock by Elton John
- Reeling in the Years by Steely Dan
- You're So Vain by Carly Simon
- Live and Let Die by Paul McCartney and Wings
- Let's Get It On by Marvin Gaye
- Space Oddity by David Bowie
- We're an American Band by Grand Funk Railroad

- Rocky Mountain High by John Denver
- Touch Me in the Morning by Diana Ross
- Drift Away by Dobie Gray

1974

- Bennie and the Jets by Elton John
- I Shot the Sheriff by Eric Clapton
- Radar Love by Golden Earring
- The Way We Were by Barbra Streisand
- Hooked on a Feeling by Blue Swede
- Tubular Bells by Mike Oldfield
- Band on the Run by Paul McCartney and Wings
- Takin' Care of Business by Bachman-Turner Overdrive
- Time in a Bottle by Jim Croce
- Waterloo by ABBA

1975

- Rhinestone Cowboy by Glen Campbell
- Black Water by The Doobie Brothers
- Lady by Styx
- Thank God I'm a Country Boy by John Denver
- Mandy by Barry Manilow
- One of These Nights by the Eagles
- How Long by Ace
- I'm Not in Love by 10cc
- Cat's in the Cradle by Harry Chapin
- Magic by Pilot

I STARTED BUYING 45s when I was in sixth or seventh grade. If memory serves, the first singles I bought were Petula Clark's

"Downtown" and The Monkeys "I'm a Believer," which turned out to be the best-selling record of 1967. Later on, I purchased "Love is Blue," by Paul Mauriat, and "Brown Sugar" by The Rolling Stones. The B-side to "Brown Sugar" was "Bitch." I didn't want to be embarrassed if my parents saw the word "bitch" on the record so I scratched it off. In high school, I was interested in collecting albums because I could read liner notes and look at cover art while I listened to records. Like many kids from my generation, I spent countless hours in my bedroom doing just that. It's too bad today's younger generation doesn't get to appreciate album cover art like my generation did. I studied the covers for hours while I listened to music. Here's a list of some of my favorite album covers:

- *Houses of the Holy* by Led Zeppelin
- *Abraxas* by Santana
- *Bat Out Of Hell* by Meatloaf
- *Can't Buy a Thrill* by Steely Dan
- *Happy Trails* by Quicksilver Messenger Service
- *Born to Run* by Bruce Springsteen
- *Never For Ever* by Kate Bush
- *Disraeli Gears* by Cream
- *Eat a Peach* by The Allman Brothers
- *Sgt. Peppers* by the Beatles
- *Full Circle* by The Doors
- *Vagabonds of the Western World* by Thin Lizzy
- *Goodbye Yellow Brick Road* by Elton John
- *The Captain and Me* by The Doobie Brothers

Two other bands that had amazing covers were Genesis and The Moody Blues. In addition, I'll include any album cover by YES, ASIA, or Uriah Heap. Roger Dean was a legend when it came to cover art and he created many of those covers.

Interestingly, the cover of *The Captain and Me* showed The

Doobie Brothers sitting at a banquet table on top of a highway overpass that hadn't yet finished construction. Or so I thought. For nearly 50 years, I thought of this cover whenever I saw a highway overpass that wasn't completed. However, I recently discovered the overpass on the cover was destroyed in the San Fernando Valley earthquake in 1971. Rockin' down the highway, indeed.

Serendipity reared its head when my family moved across town when I was in high school. The previous owners of our new house had left behind an antique console radio, which I listened to at night when I went to bed. I listened to Wolfman Jack; with his gravelly voice it seemed as though he was in the cosmos. It made me feel like there was a huge world "out there" with unlimited possibilities. Listening to Wolfman made me want to buy my own stereo.

Shortly thereafter I purchased my first stereo, a Sony console with a built-in turntable, cassette deck, and speakers. I couldn't believe how superior the sound was compared to my cheap turntable. I heard sounds I couldn't hear before. I bought Sennheiser headphones so I could listen to music when I went to bed without fear of waking anybody up. The headphones seemed to give the music additional clarity. I used my headphones every night until my ears got hot from the radiation. One time I forgot to turn the speaker switch off and I heard my brother yelling at me from the other side of the bedroom. I'm surprised I didn't wake up the whole block.

As soon as I bought my stereo, I began recording my albums onto cassettes so I could play them in my car. For some reason I thought TDK tapes were the best. I used 60-minute tapes because it wouldn't take me as long to fast forward or rewind to certain songs compared to 90-minute tapes. I couldn't believe I could transfer music from one medium to another. It made me feel powerful. A year or two later I upgraded to separate stereo components: Electro Voice speakers, a Pioneer SX-650 receiver, a

Technics M228X cassette deck, and a Pioneer turntable. I still have the turntable, receiver, and cassette deck in my garage and I've been thinking about hooking them up. I haven't done that in 40 years and there's nothing like the sound of vinyl. I'm excited by the prospect of playing my old records again.

I grew up in a small town where the only thing to do on Saturday nights was cruise the main drag while blasting the music as loud as humanly possible. I remember when I put new Jensen speakers in my Ford Pinto. I put in Journey's *Next* album and cranked up "Hustler." I thought I was the coolest cat in the universe. My dad came running out of the house yelling at me to turn the music down.

I can't fathom anybody listening to music more than I did in high school. I made a five-hour road trip a couple times a month to the San Francisco Bay Area to see my favorite bands perform and visit the used record stores, where we purchased dozens of records for $.25 or $.50 apiece. It was nirvana.

My two jobs in high school were washing logging trucks and working at a gas station, which allowed me to save $2,000. Like most young males, I wanted to blow it all on a car so I could impress the ladies. After all, Sammy Hagar's first royalty check was for $5100, and he spent $5000 on a Porsche, so why couldn't I?[15] However, it was not to be. My dad let me spend only $400 so I bought a 1965 Chevy Nova station wagon, standard transmission, three on the column. I was embarrassed to drive it because my friends had nicer cars. However, I had no right to complain because that car got me to San Francisco and back many times. In hindsight it was one of the best decisions my dad made for me because it allowed me to save money to go to college.

If not for Mother Nature and the reliability of my car, it's possible I could have been kicked off the tennis team in high school. During one season, I told my coach I wanted to go to a concert in San Francisco on Friday night. He told me I would no longer be on the team if I missed the match, which started at 8 AM Saturday morning. The concert ended at about midnight so I drove all night to get home at 7 A.M. During the drive, a California Highway Patrol officer pulled me over in Ukiah (I'm guessing The Doobie Brothers song with the same name was named after this small town). Evidently, I had missed a few red lights. I was so tired I could barely keep my eyes open. I told the officer I was trying to find a restaurant so I could get some coffee. He pointed out a restaurant down the road and then let me go. Thank you, sir.

It turned out I drove all night for nothing because it was raining when I arrived home so the tennis match was canceled. I went to bed and slept for 24 hours.

The road trips went by quickly because we listened to our favorite tunes. Which begs the question, what are the best songs for a road trip? Everyone has their own list, but my favorite cruising songs are my favorite songs, or new songs. After all, who doesn't want to hear their favorite songs on a road trip, one after another? This is why I'm constantly on the lookout for new music. I have a strategy on road trips where I start with dream-like songs when I leave the house and then when I hit the on-ramp to the freeway I take it up a few notches. For instance, a great song to hit the highway with is "The Wait" by the Pretenders.

Like many people, I enjoy driving alone because I get lost in the music and my life at the same time. The solitude gives me an opportunity to reflect on my life, to ask questions, and to listen for answers. It's a time to work out problems.

One of my favorite songs for a road trip is "Feels" by Giraffage, an electronic music producer. I won't go into detail here other than to suggest you listen to this song and judge for yourself. Another favorite is "Truth" by Shallou. It's otherworldly and puts me in a trance-like state where I feel like I'm in perfect harmony with the universe. And then there's Imogen

Heap's "Hide and Seek." She gets her sound by using artificial harmonies with a Digitech Vocalist Workstation and an echo effect caused from digital delay.[3] It's an extraordinary sound. I also love "Girl Crush" by Little Big Town, perhaps the best song I've heard during the last decade. These songs are the ultimate cruising songs because they have an ethereal quality to them, which allows me to daydream when I'm driving. In addition, another song I love on road trips is "Jane Says" by Jane's Addiction. It has a Caribbean flair to it and no one can sing it like Perry Farrell can. It's a unique song.

There are two qualities to a song that I value most: melody and rhythm. For instance, consider P.M. Dawn's "Set Adrift on Memory Bliss." It's one of my favorite songs of all time. It incorporates a riff from Spandau Ballet's hit "True." I enjoy the lyrics and the melody is incredibly catchy. Another great song for the road is America's "Ventura Highway," in large part due to the visceral lyrics that talk about driving in Southern California. And then there's "Baba O'Riley" by The Who. It's one of the greatest rock songs, and the opening keyboard riff is legendary. It's an anthem song that has some of the most powerful lyrics ever written. The Mamas and Papas' "California Dreaming" is another classic I enjoy on road trips because I'm usually driving in California and I'm usually dreaming as well. Plus it takes me back to the 1960s when I was a kid without a care in the world. Everything But The Girl's "Driving" is another favorite for the road because the outro includes a saxophone solo and I'm a sucker for a sax.

Another favorite is "American Dreamer" by Dead Can Dance. It begins with a beautiful acoustic intro. Very few people have heard of this band, but they wrote some classic songs that sound like they're from another galaxy. The Cure's "Love Song" is another must-have song for me on the road. The lyrics, the melody, the rhythm, and Robert Smith's voice make this one of the most iconic songs (and bands) of all time. I also enjoy Love

Unlimited's "Walkin' in the Rain With the One I Love," which might be the most romantic song I've ever heard. I like it because it makes me think of my wife. Finally, I can't think of a more inspirational song for the road than The Supremes' "Ain't No Mountain High Enough."

In my senior years, there is one genre of music that tugs at my heartstrings, takes me back to my youth, and sets my goosebumps on fire. I'm astonished by the songs country music artists (or their songwriters) create. It's hard to beat country artists when it comes to combining lyrics and powerful melodies in a chorus. One of my favorite country songs is "Are You Gonna Kiss Me or Not" by Thompson Square. The chorus is a monster. Another favorite is "Greatest Love Story" by LANCO, an emotional song that goes right to my heart. The same can be said for "There Goes My Life" by Kenny Chesney. It's a story about a young man who finds out his wife is pregnant. He feels like his life is over because he's not ready to raise a child. However, he also feels like his life is over when his daughter has grown up and leaves for college. How many parents feel the same way when their kids leave the nest? Another favorite is "Fire Away" by Chris Stapleton. There is no greater male voice in country music. I tried to play this on my guitar but my voice sounded like a mouse compared to Stapleton's voice, which sounds like a lion.

One of my favorite country artists' is Keith Urban. His song "We Were" is about young love. Truer words have never been spoken about the power and intensity that young people feel when they're in love, and the nostalgia of young love decades later. Urban's "Raise 'Em Up" is another nostalgic, emotional song that celebrates life and how lucky we are to be alive. Indeed, we should be giving thanks every day that we are still on the planet surrounded by people who love us. Another favorite is "When I Die Young" by The Band Perry. The intro is unforgettable. It's a beautiful melody on banjo and the opening lyrics are priceless. If a great song is judged by how quickly the lyrics are remembered, then this is a great song because I learned the lyrics quickly, whereas it usually takes me awhile. In terms of songs that make me feel good, "Song for Another Time" by Old Dominion falls into that category. The lyrics consist of lyrics from other great songs. It's a clever use of language and a song I keep coming back to.

When I'm on the road and I want to take it up a notch, I pull out the heavy artillery: Montrose's "Space Station #5," Aerosmith's "Sweet Emotion," or Led Zeppelin's "Black Dog." Recently, I discovered "Pali Gap/Hey Baby (New Rising Sun)" by Lukas Nelson and Promise of the Real. It's funky-blues hot. It makes me wonder, how many other incredible songs am I missing out on?

The key to listening to music on road trips is diversity, so after listening to a few hard rockers, I might transition to Marvin Gaye, Van Morrison, Jackson Browne, or Joni Mitchell. I'll also take anything by George Winston, Bruce Springsteen, Candy Dulfer, Billy Joel, Dave Mason, Tom Petty, The Doobie Brothers, Neil Young, Third Eye Blind, The Guess Who, Credence Clearwater Revival, and Crosby, Stills, Nash and Young. And of course, Motown.

WHAT GENRE most connects you to the ethereal?

For me, the answer is electronic, which includes a number of genres like trance, chill, or ambient. This music is usually made digitally with a DAW (i.e., digital audio workstation). In addition to the aforementioned "Feels" by Giraffage and "Truth" by Shallou," the following list contains some of the most beautiful, haunting, and ethereal songs I've ever heard:

- Sapient Dream by Slushii

- Feel It All Around by Washed Out
- Feel Good by Lemongrass
- Embrace by Blackmill
- Ashes to Oceans by DJ Shadow
- Porcelain by Moby
- Show Me Love by Van
- Flaws by Vancouver Sleep Clinic
- With You by Illenium
- Light by San Holo
- Caves (Samurai Remix) by Haux

Years ago, a friend asked me what actor I would choose to play my life story on the big screen. I liked the question because it made me think, since there were so many possibilities. Out of curiosity, I took an online quiz that matched me with Zendaya. The only problem is she's female. I realize I'm in touch with my feminine side, but really? In a similar vein, here's another timeless question: Which ten albums would you choose if you could only listen to those albums for the rest of your days?

This is a brutal question to answer since there are so many to choose from. Diversity would be critical, so I would choose any album by Enya, John Coltrane, Joni Mitchell, Van Morrison and Bruce Springsteen, as well as George Winston's *Autumn,* Billy Joel's *The Stranger,* Supertramp's *Even in the Quietest Moments,* and Everything But The Girl's *Worldwide* and *The Language of Life*.

I had three favorite albums when I was in high school: Journey's debut album, Montrose's debut album, and The Doobie Brothers' *The Captain and Me.* Journey's debut album was stunning. For lack of a better description, it was progressive rock, completely different than their later releases when Steve Perry came on board. Many Journey fans are not aware this album exists. In particular, the song "In the Morning Day" was one of my favorites and that's before guitarist Neil Schon comes in with an outrageous solo toward the end. Absolute goosebumps. I'll never forget the first time I heard this album, it gave me chills.

Montrose's debut album was *the* hard rock album at my high school when it was released in 1973. It contained some of the greatest rock songs ever: "Space Station Number #5," "Bad Motor Scooter," "Rock Candy," "Make It Last," and "Rock the Nation." I learned the main riffs to "Rock Candy" and "Make It Last," and I get a kick out of playing them. Never in my wildest dreams did I imagine I would ever be able to play those songs when I was in high school. The thought never occurred to me, and I still wonder why. I loved music so much that it would've been a natural transition for me to learn how to play an instrument.

The Doobie Brothers' *The Captain and Me* begins with "Natural Thing," "Long Train Runnin," and "China Grove." It doesn't get better than that. The album also contains "Without You," a classic rocker with one of my favorite solos. I can't tell you how much time I spent in high school playing air-guitar to this solo. Additional stellar songs on this album include "Ukiah," "South City Midnight Lady," and "The Captain and Me." I wore this album out in high school.

Here's something else I think about in my spare time. What male and female singers have the most recognizable voices? In order to have the most recognizable voice, the singer needs to be well-known to the masses. I would love to see a survey of this because there are many worthy candidates. However, the survey would be generational because some people who vote might not have been around 40 or 50 years ago to hear the iconic singers of that time. Regardless, here are the candidates for the most recognizable voice during my lifetime:

- Judy Garland
- John Denver

- Loretta Lynn
- Art Garfunkel
- Barry White
- Rod Stewart
- Diana Ross
- Elton John
- Adele
- Bjork
- Ray Charles
- Ann Wilson
- James Brown
- Roy Orbison
- Billy Joel
- Jim Morrison
- Jimi Hendrix
- Chris Martin
- Marvin Gaye
- Celine Dion
- Madonna
- Gwen Stefani
- John Lennon
- Dean Martin
- Andy Williams
- Tina Turner
- Smokey Robinson
- Leon Russell
- Linda Ronstadt
- Mick Jagger
- Billie Holiday
- Nat King Cole
- David Bowie
- Louis Armstrong
- Barbra Streisand
- Prince

- Frank Sinatra
- Joe Cocker
- Bob Dylan
- Robert Plant
- Freddie Mercury
- Janis Joplin
- James Taylor
- Bruce Springsteen
- Tom Waits
- Aretha Franklin
- Whitney Houston
- Otis Redding
- Mariah Carey
- Bob Marley
- Pavarotti
- Luther Vandross
- Patsy Cline
- Johnny Mathis
- Paul McCartney
- Stevie Wonder
- Tony Bennett
- Emmylou Harris
- Michael Jackson
- Bing Crosby
- Ella Fitzgerald
- Sam Cooke
- Van Morrison
- Little Richard
- Jerry Lee Lewis
- Johnny Cash
- Elvis Presley
- Hank Williams
- Willie Nelson
- Dolly Parton

- Joan Baez
- Carly Simon
- Joni Mitchell
- Stevie Nicks
- John Fogerty
- Steven Tyler

Who would you choose?

It would be difficult to argue against Bob Dylan or Paul McCartney, global icons whose voices the masses have heard countless times. I would put Johnny Cash right there as well but he is not well-known globally. My female choice would be Stevie Nicks because I can identify her voice immediately. There is no other voice like hers. The same holds true for John Fogerty.

And perhaps the most interesting question of all:

What song best defines your life?

It could be your favorite song, although I suspect for some individuals that won't be the case. Would it be a song that encapsulates everything you've been through, where you are, and where you're going? A song that best describes your philosophy of life? A song that makes you happy? A song that brings back strong memories? Maybe it's a song with meaningful lyrics that speak to you? Perhaps it's a song that has served you well throughout your life and acts as a personal guide?

My choice would be John Hiatt's "Have a Little Faith in Me." It expresses how I feel about my wife, as well as how all human beings feel about each other. Everyone wants people to have faith in them. It's a universal feeling. We all need to rely on each other; too many individuals are afraid or unwilling to ask for help. Many people believe asking for help is a sign of weakness, when it is a sign of strength. Not only are the lyrics poignant and meaningful, but Hiatt absolutely kills the vocals. It's my all-time favorite vocal by a male. I saw him perform an unplugged version with his piano as the only accompaniment. It was stunning. Nobody can sing like this guy.

Here's one last question: "Which male and female artist would you choose if you could only listen to those artists for the rest of your life?" My choice would be Springsteen and Joni Mitchell. Nobody's ever done it better. And speaking of Springsteen, one of my friends saw his last concert at Winterland in December 1978, just two weeks prior to it's closing. The Boss threw his cherry silk shirt into the crowd and she walked away with it that night.

Finally, there is one artist who may be one of the most talented musicians I've ever seen. His name is Mike Masse. He plays extraordinary covers of famous songs. I don't know of any other artist who can do what he does. His talent is stunning. Check out his website at www.mikemasse.com

CHAPTER THIRTEEN

THE ETERNAL QUEST

"I would teach children music, physics, and philosophy; but most importantly music, for the patterns in music and all the arts are the keys to learning"[1] Plato

TWENTY YEARS ago some friends and I decided to make a list of our top songs of all-time. I went to the local record stores to go through all of the albums to make sure I didn't miss any songs. All I had to do was look at the cover of an album to remember whether or not there was a song on it that I loved. It was excruciating trying to rank the songs. This was 20 years ago so my list would be different now, since musical tastes change. My top song was "People People," by Tommy Bolin. Bolin was a member of the James Gang and Deep Purple before he put out two amazing solo albums: *Teaser* and *Private Eyes*. The albums combined elements from rock, reggae, jazz, and Latin. "People People" begins with intense lyrics, about as raw as you can get. There's something about the song that makes me feel as though I'm spending a day on the ocean. The song makes me happy and sad. Bolin was one of my heroes in high school and college before he died, and I was lucky enough to see him in concert at Winterland in San Francisco a month before he passed. He was an underrated guitar player and his two solo albums are among the best of all time. And it's no wonder, because the list of musicians who played on his solo albums included David Foster, Jan Hammer, Phil Collins, Prairie Prince, Jeff Porcaro, David Sanborn, and Michael Walden, among others.[2] Songs like "Dreamer," "Wild Dogs," "Post Toastee," and "Bustin' Out for Rosey" stand up well to the test of time. His sound was exotic with many textures. Like I said earlier, I love the sound of a saxophone; throw a world-class guitarist and legendary keyboardists into the mix and you have greatness.

When I was a young man, a friend let me listen to Bolin's "Post Toastee" on a new stereo he had recently installed in his car. The song has a huge bass drum, one of the deepest I've ever heard. It sounded like an eruption. I don't know how Bolin got his sound on these two albums. It was unique and it's a shame more people have not heard his solo work.

THE MUSIC we choose to listen to depends on how we feel at the time. For instance, somebody jacked up on amphetamines probably would not choose to listen to the Carpenters. Likewise, if I asked college students to list their favorite songs after drinking a six pack, chances are their state of mind would influence their lists.

I lived in the dorms my first year in college where I met friends who had extensive record collections. There were nights when my friends went to parties while I stayed in my room recording like a madman. I still have boxes of these old cassettes, although I haven't listened to them in decades.

A similar situation occurred 30 years later when Napster went out of business. I downloaded as many songs as I could the last 24 hours they were open. It was a digital gold rush. I was able to justify it because I had spent so much money on music prior to that time. Reflecting back, it wasn't fair to the artists and I would not do that again.

During one summer in the late 1970s, a few friends and I stayed in our college town. There was something about being with a handful of friends in an empty town for the whole summer. It's a feeling you can only experience when you're young. It was a time when friends meant everything and the possibilities were limitless. The days were hot and we lived on the water, floating down the local river on inner tubes. But what I remember most is hanging out every night and listening to the same album. The album was *Remember the Future* by Nektar. I don't know why it was that album, but it was. I never got tired of it; indeed, it was comforting to hear the same music night after night. At the end of those nights, I went back to my apartment and listened to Warren Zevon's "Lawyers, Guns and Money" on my headphones to cap the night. Instead of having a drink for a nightcap, I had a song.

In college, I began listening to Rush, Supertramp, and Led Zeppelin. With all due respect to The Rolling Stones and the Beatles (the latter are really in a league of their own), I believe Led Zeppelin is the greatest rock 'n roll band in history. Jack Black got it right when he gave the induction speech for Zeppelin during their Kennedy Center Honors ceremony. He called them, "The greatest rock 'n roll band of all time." Many of their songs seamlessly transition from ballad to blues to heavy rock and then back again. George Harrison once asked Jimmy Page why they never wrote slow songs, so Page wrote "The Rain Song."[3] There has never been a more gorgeous and haunting song by any rock band, thanks to the alternative tuning (DGCGCD) Page used.[4] One aspect that set Zeppelin apart is that a case can be made that each of the four band members were considered one of the most proficient at their craft. In addition, lead singer Robert Plant's primal scream was legendary and one that other rock singers aspire to. To give you an idea of Led Zeppelin's popularity, when tickets went on sale in 2007 for their reunion show at the O2 in London, the computer server broke because they had 20 million requests for tickets at the rate of 80,000 per minute.[5] Truly, a communication breakdown.

Several college students I worked with over the years told me their favorite band was Led Zeppelin, which I found interesting since the students were not even alive when Zeppelin was in its heyday. One student even named her first son Zeppelin, which I thought was a great name for a boy since it has a mythic aura about it. Two students agreed with me that there's never been a better rock song then "Babe I'm Gonna Leave You." Page does some tremendous acoustic work as the song builds to its crescendo. I've been working on the introduction off-and-on for three years and I still cannot play it in time. Maybe one day.

I graduated from college in 1980. A year later MTV was born and we watched videos for hours. Some of the artists I remember watching included Styx, Blondie, Men at Work, Rod Stewart, The Pretenders, The Cars, Tom Petty, Pat Benatar, Fleetwood Mac, Robert Palmer, Phil Collins, and The Who. A couple of years later, Michael Jackson's *Thriller* exploded onto the scene with his "Beat It" video. I'd never seen anybody dance like he did, so suave and debonair.

IT'S BEEN SAID BEFORE, but music inspires me. It gives me hope and makes me happy. If I heard a good song on the radio when I was a kid, I would immediately call the radio station to find out the title of the song so I could go buy it. The same held true when I was a sales representative in my 20s. I could be in Colorado or Utah and if I heard a song I liked on the radio, I looked for a pay phone so I could call the station to get the song title. I had to have the song that day. However, there were times when I called a radio station and the DJ either didn't answer or could not tell me the name of the song, so I was left to my own devices. This involved listening to the station as much as I could while I was still in that particular city, hoping they would play the song again. I also tried to memorize the lyrics as much as possible so I could repeat them to friends, hoping they would recognize the song. I also recounted the lyrics to employees at restaurants or stores in the city where I heard the song. Some employees would go to great lengths to try to find out, even calling the company that provided their recorded music.

Which brings me to cell phones. My wife kids me because I'm old-school when it comes to technology. I never had a cell phone until 2017, when my wife loaned me one of her old phones. I can count on one hand the number of times I've used it, as months will go by and I don't think about it, although if I remember I will take it with me when I go out of town, which is almost never. I simply don't want to let a cell phone control my dopamine levels and get addicted. A college student once told me the first thing she did every morning was check her cell phone. I was curious so I began asking other students if they did the same thing. Every student I asked told me it was the first thing they did in the morning. If that's not an addiction, I don't know what is. The students could not believe I could survive without a cell phone. "How do you stay connected," one asked. I told her, "I never feel more connected than when I play guitar."

Given my indifference toward cell phones, imagine my surprise when I discovered there are apps that can identify songs and artists after listening for only a few seconds. I asked my wife if she could get an app for me, and now it's the only thing I use my cell phone for. So after a lifetime of calling radio stations to find out the names of songs, or asking employees at various business enterprises, "Do you know the name of that song?" I can now use a cell phone. Amazing. I've used the app no more than a dozen times and only twice did it fail to identify a song. Once was during the HBO series *Hard Knocks* in 2019, a show that focuses on one NFL football team every preseason. At one point, a player was drumming while a song played in the background.[6] The song was so hot I had to get it, but it didn't come up on my app. I was frustrated because we can put a man on the moon and map DNA, but I can't get the name of one song. The name of the song has been posted online by people who believe they know the song, but none of the songs sound like it. Perhaps the clip was created for that episode, I don't know. I could write to the producer of that segment to try to get it but that's too much of a hassle for me during my senior years, although when I was a young man I probably would've done that.

I AM amazed by the creativity in music because it seems like all the chord progressions and melodies would have been used by now. But the groundbreaking songs just keep coming. Just when I think that every melody in the universe has been used, a new song or artist pops up that sounds unlike anything I've heard before. Take "Oh My God" by Michael Franti and Spearhead. It's a song about social justice. I was hooked the first time I heard it in 2002. The combination of the melody and lyrics make this a Top 10 all-time favorite song for me. Gary Clark is another example. I recently watched him perform "Pearl Cadillac." He sings like Marvin Gaye and plays guitar like Prince. It's a potent combination. Or take a song like Rihanna's (featuring Drake) "Work." It was unique from anything I heard before. And then there's Oliver Tank, whose music sounds like it's from another world. Check out "Up All Night," "I Love You," and "The Last Time."

I've always been on a quest for new music, whether from

films, satellite radio, televised concerts, rock 'n roll documentaries, my former college students, television shows like *American Idol* or *The Voice*, or music in commercials or television shows (e.g., *Grey's Anatomy*). I also enjoy theme songs from shows like *Homeland* and *The Sopranos*. I'll never forget watching the last episode of the second season of *The Sopranos* as The Rolling Stones' "Thru and Thru" played in the background. That was one of the most powerful moments I've seen on television. In addition, Josh Ritter's "Homecoming" was the perfect song to close out season two of *Billions*. When I was a kid, I also liked theme songs from *Bonanza, Bewitched, The Brady Bunch, All in the Family, The Dick Van Dyke Show, The Jeffersons, I Dream of Jeannie, The Beverly Hillbillies, The Andy Griffith Show, Sanford and Son,* and *I Love Lucy*. Theme songs were comforting and allowed me to escape reality for a brief moment in time.

ONE OF THE advantages of working with college students is they continually turned me on to new music. We had many conversations about music over the course of the last decade, so I decided to ask several former students (ages 25-30) what they liked most about music. I also asked them to name their favorite songs, albums, artists, and genres. Finally, I wanted to know how much they listen to music every day. Interestingly, they listed 18 different genres with only one genre (Pop) occurring twice:

- Indie Rock
- Punk Rock
- Alternative
- Bedroom Rock
- Bossa Nova
- Calypso

- Big-Band Jazz
- Classical
- Celtic Pop
- Religious
- Rock/Light Metal
- R&B, Hip-Hop
- Soul
- House
- Downtempo
- Indie

On average, each student listens to almost four hours of music a day, much of it background music. As far as their favorite songs, here's the list:

- Come Down by Anderson.Paak
- Humble by Kendrick Lamar
- Tennessee Whiskey by Chris Stapleton
- Electricity by Dua Lipa
- Proud Mary by Tina Turner
- You Make Me Feel Like a Natural Woman by Aretha Franklin
- Coming Home by Leon
- Bridges
- Closer by POWERS
- The Seed 2.0 by the Roots
- Think by (Sandy) Alex G
- This Must Be the Place by Talking Heads
- 96th St. by Emily Yacina
- Season Two Episode Three by Glass Animals
- The Sixth Station by Joe Hisaishi

As far as favorite artists, their list includes the above artists plus:

- Michael Jackson
- Logic
- Billie Elish
- Crooked Colors
- Maggie Rogers
- The Black Keys
- Mac DeMarco
- Mazzy Star
- Alvvays
- Beach Fossils
- Brazilian Girls
- Cocteau Twins
- Japanese Breakfast
- The Cure
- The Smashing Pumpkins
- The Shins
- Prince
- The Smiths
- Sonic Youth
- Yeah Yeah Yeahs
- Joe Hisaishi
- Yurima
- The Doobie Brothers
- Vocaloid / Anime Openings

Given the vast majority of songs and artists on their lists are from their generation, and the fact that only a handful of songs are from my generation, is it fair to say that most baby boomers' favorite songs would stem from their younger days as well? The effects of aging and decreasing dopamine levels in the brain surely play a role. Additionally, young adults are probably not exposed to music from previous generations as much as they are from artists from their generation.

And what do the students like most about music? They like

that music brings back memories, reminds them of friendships, and helps them to be patient. Music also allows them to appreciate life and to feel a sense of belonging. Music makes them feel present, has the ability to ease their burdens, and can help them get completely lost. Music provides them with a range of emotions, exposes them to culture, and broadens their worldview. They also like how music allows them to get outside of their heads. When they can't articulate how they feel, they can find a song that can. They enjoy the transcendent quality of music, how one minute they feel like they're roller-skating in a disco ballroom and the next minute they're sailing on the ocean.

CHAPTER FOURTEEN

"LOVES TO HIT CONCERTS"

"Music is my higher power."[1] Oliver James

MUSIC ALLOWS us to connect with each other. Perhaps that is its greatest gift. When I went to concerts as a young man, I felt a kinship with other fans because we shared something that was intangible. I thought, "These are my people, they get it, they understand why this band is so good." Like many naïve adolescents, I also believed I had a connection with the musicians because I read their interviews in *Cream* and *Circus*, so I must've known them, right? Let's chalk that up to the naivety of youth, but I did feel lucky to be able to watch my favorite bands live.

When I was in college, the resident assistant in my dormitory told me she got a kick out of my application to live in the dorms. According to her, I listed one of my hobbies as, "Loves to hit concerts." I guess it worked because she paired me with another music lover who turned me on to Supertramp and Led Zeppelin.

What is it about the impact of seeing live music that makes such a huge impression on teenagers and young adults? Is it the nexus of great music, fun with friends, the unlimited potential of youth, and the intimacy of seeing your favorite artists up close? You are part of something that is a once-in-a-lifetime experience with like-minded fans (after all, the band will only play once in your location on that night). Forget about Christmas morning, the most exciting time of my adolescence occurred when I was in high school, anticipating my favorite bands just prior to when they walked on stage. The lights went out, I saw the outlines of bodies walking on stage, the lights went on, the band kicked in, and it was mayhem. There was nothing like it. Going to concerts made me feel independent and powerful, especially coming from a small town in a rural community and suddenly being among thousands of screaming fans at Winterland or the Cow Palace in San Francisco.

I lost count of the number of concerts I went to in high school. Every Saturday, a local supermarket would get the inserts for the Sunday San Francisco Chronicle newspaper. The actual paper arrived the next morning but I was at that market on Saturdays to buy the Datebook (i.e., the "pink section") because it listed the new shows. I waited all week in anticipation and I called for tickets the *minute* they went on sale. Once I scored the tickets, I felt secure in the knowledge that I was one of the privileged few to be able to attend the show.

I saw dozens of bands when I was in high school and college. Here's the list of bands I can remember after nearly 50 years:

- Electric Light Orchestra
- Robin Trower
- Hush
- Bob Seger
- Blue Oyster Cult
- Aerosmith
- KISS
- Mahogany Rush

- Eddie Money
- Derringer
- Foghat
- UFO
- Bad Company
- Rush
- Thee Image
- Cheap Trick
- Yesterday and Today
- Little Feat
- Link Wray
- Hot Tuna
- Earthquake
- Gary Wright
- The Tubes
- Rory Gallagher
- Elvin Bishop
- Wishbone Ash
- Tommy Bolin
- Greg Kihn
- Dr. Feelgood
- Cold Blood
- Montrose
- Journey
- YES
- Kansas
- Ace
- Poco
- Bachman-Turner Overdrive
- Santana
- Fleetwood Mac
- Beach Boys
- Chicago
- Nils Lofgren

- Dave Mason
- Tower of Power
- Jeff Beck
- Status Quo
- Heart
- The Steve Miller Band
- Atlanta Rhythm Section
- Foreigner
- Eagles
- Peter Frampton

Some of my best memories include Day on the Greens at the Oakland Coliseum because they were held during the day in the sun. One Day on the Green stood out because a friend of mine and I took two girls. We were naïve and excited at the possibilities. We stayed at one of the girl's grandparents on the way so nothing happened. When we got to the concert, they ditched us and we never saw them again until the concert was over. It was disappointing, even more so considering that we believed the bands that played (Chicago and the Beach Boys) were going to put them in the mood for romance, as if we even knew what that was at that age. Alas, it was not to be. I ran into both girls a few years later when I was in college and the old feelings came back a little bit. We all had significant others so we had a pleasant conversation and moved on.

I saw all the bands I wanted to in high school with the exception of Pink Floyd, The Who, and The Rolling Stones. Years later, I was able to cross off Pink Floyd and The Rolling Stones from my list. And even though I wasn't into Led Zeppelin yet, I had the opportunity to see them at a Day on the Green but they had to cancel because lead singer Robert Plant was recovering from a car accident.

Concerts leave us with unique memories. For example, I saw a Blue Oyster Cult show when I was in college. I was leaning against the stage when the drummer threw his drumsticks to the crowd. My friend and I grabbed one drumstick at the same time. We both wanted it so we decided to play basketball one-on-one to determine who would get the drumstick. I can't tell you how important it was to me to have that drumstick in my possession. I wanted it bad, and I was going to take no prisoners. I played basketball quite a bit as a young man but I hadn't played in awhile so I practiced before the big game. He was an athlete in high school and he was five inches taller than me. However, I knew it was all over after my first possession because I could score at will. The drumstick was mine and I still have it.

Sometimes it's the journey to a concert that gives us everlasting memories. During one trip to a concert in San Francisco, a friend and I got into a slight fender bender on the Golden Gate Bridge. Once we got off the bridge, we looked at the damage on his Volkswagen bug and discovered he had a huge dent in his front fender. He simply pulled the dent out with his hands and we were merrily on our way. There was no worry about the state of his car, or filing insurance claims, or the resale value. Oh, to be young again.

We arrived at Winterland at noon for an 8 P.M. show. We always did this because we wanted to be first in line. As soon as the doors opened we ran inside to the front so we could lean against the stage. During the concert, a guy next to me started wailing about with a pair of scissors in his hand. I was afraid he was going to stab me. He did hit my arm a couple of times but didn't do any damage. But did I move away from him? Of course not, I would've lost my spot in the front row! Priorities.

Fast-forward to 2008, when I saw The Doobie Brothers perform in my hometown. I was 51 years old but it felt like I was in high school again. I was in the second row when I felt a tap on my shoulder. I turned around and it was an old friend who had gone with me to a Doobie Brothers show when we were in high school. Such is the circle of life. I've never seen a band have so much fun. Tom Johnston looked like he had the time of his life that night and the band absolutely killed it. I thought about hanging around after the show to try to meet the band, but I didn't.

The best concerts I've seen on television are usually the induction ceremonies for the Rock 'n Roll Hall of Fame, primarily because many inductees are artists from my generation. Some of them haven't played together for years, so they reunite for one last time to play a few of their old hits. As I write this, The Doobie Brothers are set to be inducted this year, so I'm looking forward to that.

The single greatest musical moment I've seen on television was Heart's rendition of Led Zeppelin's "Stairway to Heaven" during the 2012 Kennedy Center Honors as Robert Plant, Jimmy Page, and John Paul Jones watched from the balcony.[2] "Stairway to Heaven" is one of the greatest rock songs of all-time, so it took a lot of guts for Heart to cover that song in front of such a prestigious audience, including the three surviving members of Zeppelin. Ann Wilson nailed the vocals, Plant had tears in his eyes, and Page's expression said it all. Clearly, they were enjoying themselves. Suddenly, a choir appeared from out of nowhere and took the song into the heavens. I still get chills watching it.

Speaking of Ann Wilson, one of the best concerts I've seen was in 2001 at Lake Konocti Resort in Northern California. The band consisted of Ann Wilson, Todd Rundgren, John Entwistle, and Alan Parsons, among others. They played covers of some of the Beatles' songs and a mix of their own songs. I felt honored to see all those legends on the stage at once.

Another performance I will never forget was RAIN (a Beatles tribute band) on New Year's Eve in Chico (my college town) around 1979. It was one of the happiest nights of my life. Not only did the band sound like the Beatles, they looked like them as well. The crowd went crazy when they came out in their Sgt.

Pepper's outfits. I was young, my life was ahead of me, it was New Year's Eve, and I was in college with my friends listening to a fabulous band. What could be better than that? The only other time in my life when I felt that way was during Pioneer Days, an annual celebration of the history of Chico. Part of the celebration included a concert that took place on the football field next to the tennis courts where my friend and I played that day. It was extremely hot and we were covered in sweat. I felt healthy, happy, and privileged to have such a good life. At that time, I knew life would never be better than at that moment. And I was right. For 25 years. Then I married the love of my life, which turned out to be the best day of my life. I remember eating dinner at the Bellagio in Las Vegas on my wedding night and thinking, "I've never felt so happy." I was high for months afterward.

During my late 30s, my favorite band was Third Eye Blind. I took a few of my seventh-grade students to see them at The Fillmore in San Francisco in the late 1990s. It was the students' first concert and it was highly impressionable on them. I'll never forget the look on their faces when the band launched into "Narcolepsy" after the intro. The crowd went nuts, jumping up and down in unison with the rhythm of the song. It was madness and we were right in the middle of it. The energy was incredible. My students had never seen anything like it. I also took students to see the Gin Blossoms, Cracker, and the Spin Doctors at the Greek Theatre in Berkeley. When I dropped them off at home, they said, "Thank you for the best night of my life!" In addition, I took students to see Rancid at The Fillmore, which was the first time I saw a live mosh pit. The energy was amazing. A couple of my students participated and they were absolutely drenched in sweat afterward. I only hoped they would shower before coming to school the next day. Forget about teaching them mathematics; I was trying to teach them the power of rock 'n' roll, not unlike Jack Black in *School of Rock*.

Every time I went to a large concert, I wondered what it would feel like to have the best seat in the house, first row on the aisle. It finally happened when I was in my twenties working as a sales representative for a toy company. One of my customers had a BASS outlet in his store. He was able to get me two tickets in the first row on the aisle to see Phil Collins at the Oakland Arena. I went with my best friend at the time but missed the encores because I had an anxiety attack and had to leave. It was disappointing.

My disappointment was exacerbated after I scored great seats for a couple of friends to a Huey Lewis New Year's Eve show. I was excited for them to see one of their favorite artists up close. I felt awful when they told me their seats were actually behind the stage. They had trusted me and I let them down.

Finally, I'll mention one concert I went to when I was in my 20s because it was the only time I went to a concert alone. It was after Madonna's first album came out. She had a fresh sound and her songs were catchy, had great choruses, and were imminently danceable. Songs like "Holiday," "Borderline," and "Lucky Star" were great pop songs. She performed at a smaller venue in San Francisco and none of my friends would've been caught dead going to her concert, so I went by myself. I could not pass up the opportunity to see her. It was a great show but I felt out of place among the thousands of teenage "material" girls who wore bras outside of their shirts.

I wish I would've preserved the T-shirts I bought from all the shows I saw, but I wore them out in college. My favorite was a tie-dye Pink Floyd shirt that had several holes in it, which I wore when I met my ex-girlfriend's parents. I also wore army fatigue and flip-flops, and I hadn't shaved in days/weeks. I must've looked like a bum, but I wasn't going to change. Wearing that shirt was a badge of honor.

Speaking of fashion, when I was in high school I purchased a pair of shiny blue satin pants that would've made the New York

Dolls proud. I actually wore them to school one day, but I changed them at lunch because of the strange looks that came my way. It was too much for a high school located in a small, rural, conservative town. They weren't quite ready for the glam scene yet.

I also regret not buying psychedelic posters the venues sold at the shows I went to. There was some amazing artwork on those posters, in addition to listing the bands that played that night. However, I can't complain because in 2019 I received a gift that took my breath away. It's a picture of Bruce Springsteen and his late saxophonist Clarence Clemons from the *Born to Run* cover. It hangs on the wall just outside my office. I look at it every day for inspiration before I play.

Speaking of great photos, a friend of mine took a photo of Neil Schon (guitarist for Journey) when we were standing next to the stage at a Journey concert back around 1975. Schon is on his back with his knees bent so his ankles are around his hips. I always believed that photo could win an award in *Rolling Stone Magazine.* Maybe one day?

CHAPTER FIFTEEN

GREATEST FRONT MAN

"The best music... is essentially there to provide you something to face the world with."[1] Bruce Springsteen

HAVE you ever been inspired by famous artists? If so, how did they inspire you?

The greatest summer of my life was in 1975, after I graduated from high school. I flew back to New Jersey to visit my relatives. My cousin and I went to concerts at the Spectrum in Philadelphia, where we saw YES, Ace, Kansas, Poco, and Bachman - Turner Overdrive. She also introduced me to the music of Bruce Springsteen and David Bowie. Springsteen was from Jersey and I never heard of him until she showed me one of his albums. Now, remember the scene at the beginning of the film *Almost Famous* when William Miller thumbs through the albums his sister left for him, iconic albums by Bob Dylan, Jimi Hendrix, the Beach Boys, The Who, Joni Mitchell, and Led Zeppelin?[2] Well, I had the same feeling when I saw Springsteen's cover. I thought "Who is this guy that everybody on the East Coast was talking about?" It would take me 40 years before I realized a few things.

First, Springsteen is a force of nature, a legendary musician, and one of the greatest songwriters rock 'n roll has ever seen. Second, he is without question the greatest "front man" who's ever lived. Actually, the term does not do him justice. Some argue that "front man" should be limited to those who are strictly lead singers (e.g., Robert Plant or Jim Morrison), but if the lead singer also plays instruments, he's still fronting the band and thus is a front man. With all due respect to other front men, Springsteen plays three instruments, has been known to play for three hours a night, sings every song like it's his last, leads one of the greatest bands in the world, has a voice that epitomizes grit, determination, and the hardship of life, and writes emotional and poignant songs that define the human condition. And let's not forget 135 million albums sold, 20 Grammy Awards, a Tony Award, two Golden Globes, an Oscar, Kennedy Center Honors, the Presidential Medal of Freedom, and induction into the Rock and Roll Hall of Fame and the Songwriters Hall of Fame.[3] Has there ever been another musician who has accomplished so much? Plus, I haven't seen anybody have more fun playing for his fans.

I recently watched an old E Street Band show they played in Barcelona, Spain. Toward the end of "She's the One," the band suddenly quit playing for a count or two and then started up again. Talk about a band dialed in. But that's the type of chemistry they have because they've played together for decades. Indeed, they are among a handful of bands who can claim to be the greatest American band. After all, how many American bands have sold over 100 million albums, played for five decades, and are still relevant today?

Springsteen does everything to the best of his ability. For instance, he worked on his autobiography for seven years.[4] Who does that? The Boss does, that's who. Not only that, but in 2019 he played a series of sold-out shows on Broadway where he effortlessly told stories from his autobiography while backing himself up on his acoustic. I was stunned as I watched and listened. It was an emotional powerhouse of a performance. I never saw anything like it. Along with Bob Dylan, his ability to convey the vicissitudes of the human condition is unsurpassed. And let's not forget *Blinded by the Light*, the 2019 film (based on a true story) about a Pakistani boy living in the UK who finds inspiration via Springsteen's music.[5] Out of all the musical artists who inspire the masses, karma and cosmic forces chose Springsteen to be the one artist to build a major motion picture around.

For all of these reasons, Springsteen inspires me.

I was surprised when I read Springsteen's autobiography to discover he used to visit his parents in San Mateo, California, which is in the San Francisco Bay Area. That's where I lived when I was a young man, and I used to visit Hillsdale Mall, which is evidently where his mom used to work. I Googled his parents' address and found out I used to live a stone's throw away. I was a teacher at that time and two of my students lived right across the street from his parents. My students' parents had me over for dinner one evening, but even if I saw him on the street it wouldn't have registered because he wasn't a national icon yet.

I've always been fascinated by what it would feel like to be the best in the world at something, anything. How did Springsteen get to be the best front man out of seven billion people on the planet? Practice, practice, and practice. Now, how do I know this? Because of the autobiographies I read by Springsteen, Alice Cooper, Joe Perry, Elton John, Roger Daltrey, David Crosby, Neil Young, Keith Richards, and Sammy Hagar, as well as biographies on Tom Petty, Jimmy Page, and Frank Sinatra. If there is one commonality among music legends, it is the amount of work and persistence it took to "make it." There were no overnight sensations, at least until the Internet and televised singing competitions came into existence. Famous musicians started playing at a young age and played thousands of gigs. There was no substitute for hard work.

As you can imagine, there were several tales of excess and debauchery in the autobiographies I read. However, one story stood out. As a former golfer, I was shocked to learn that Alice Cooper shot a 73 at Pine Valley, which consistently rates as the best golf course in America.[6] It's not an easy course by any means and according to Cooper (who had witnesses) he was on fire that day. Indeed, while most amateur golfers playing Pine Valley would be living out Cooper's "Welcome to My Nightmare," school was out for Alice that day.

MANY ROCK LEGENDS were first exposed to rock 'n roll when they saw Elvis Presley or the Beatles on *The Ed Sullivan Show* in the 1950s or 1960s, including Springsteen, Chrissie Hynde, Tom Petty, Nancy Wilson, Gene Simmons, Joe Perry, and Richie Sambora.[7] After that, all they could think about was getting a guitar. When they finally had their first guitar, they played as much as possible. Many of them wanted an electric guitar, but they couldn't afford one so they had to start with an acoustic. However, in hindsight this was good for them because beginners should always start with an acoustic. Why? Because lead guitarists usually play rhythm more than they play lead. Too many kids begin on electric and all they want to do is shred, play a screaming solo, or finger tap like Eddie Van Halen. They would be much better off if they started on an acoustic and learned how to play rhythm and maintain tempo.

Many rock 'n roll legends followed their passion even though some of their parents, friends, and teachers were not supportive. Roger Daltrey's high school English teacher told him he would never amount to anything. His music teacher also told him he wasn't going anywhere in life.[8] Imagine if you were a parent in the early 1960s and your son told you he wanted to play rock 'n roll for a living. Very few people were making a living doing that at that point.

So, what kind of guitar did some of the legends first play? Before Jimi Hendrix even had a guitar, he played single notes on a ukulele that only had one string.[9] He played Elvis Presley songs, including "Hound Dog."[10] His first guitar was an acoustic that cost five dollars.[11] Bruce Springsteen's first guitar was purchased at a Western Auto Appliance Store for $18.95. Later on, he traded up to a $60 Kent.[4] And talk about serendipity, when Jimmy Page's family moved to a new house when he was 13, the previous owner had left a guitar in the house. It was a Spanish guitar and Page learned how to play chords on it. Later on his dad bought him a Hofner President f-hole.[12] Joe Perry paid $12.95 for his first guitar, a Silvertone.[13] Sammy Hagar's first guitar was also a Silvertone, while Brad Paisley began with a Sears Danelectro Silvertone, which included an amp.[14][15]

Some musicians actually made their first guitar. Daltrey made his first guitar out of plywood when he was a teenager and played it until it fell apart. His uncle helped him construct a second guitar, which he carried with him everywhere he went.[8] This is the story of many musicians. They played as much as they could and practiced in their bedroom for days on end. Their passion reminds me of Pistol Pete Maravich, one of my sports heroes when I was growing up. He took a basketball with him wherever he went so he could practice dribbling. He dribbled out of the car window when his parents drove slowly around town, and he also sat on the aisle in movie theaters so he could dribble.[16] There's a reason he was one of the greatest ball handlers. It's because he put the work in. The same is true for musicians. To reach the top, you have to put the work in. In Springsteen's autobiography, he talked about how nervous he was before his first big show. But he was reassured by the fact that he had played thousands of gigs. He knew he had the experience.[4]

Let's compare the desire and work ethic in the above scenario to today's younger generation. The owner of a local music store told me he sold several guitars at the beginning of every academic year. Shortly thereafter, students return their guitars because they realize they aren't going to be rock stars overnight. It requires work, perseverance, and commitment to learn how to play. Is this a statement for today's youth? I don't know, but I can tell you when I asked a class how many students had tried to play guitar, almost everyone raised their hand. When I asked how many of them still played, all the hands went down. In today's world of immediate gratification, could it be that some young adults are not willing to engage in delayed gratification and sacrifice time on something that yields little initial payback? After all, they could be spending their time on Instagram or Facebook. Or, they could be a social media influencer. That said, I know plenty of young adults who have a tremendous work ethic.

After I played for a year, I put a note in the college bulletin notifying students I was starting a guitar club. I had no business being a guitar instructor at the time. Rather, I was simply trying to inspire students to play. I believed I could show them a couple of easy chords so they could begin to play simple songs. Out of 8,000 students, only two showed up. One was an experienced player. I showed him the intro lick to Bon Jovi's "Wanted Dead or Alive." He came back the following week and had it down. Meanwhile, I'd been working on it for months and still couldn't play it at the required tempo. It made me happy that a hack like me could teach him something. Hopefully he won't forget the old guy who taught him that lick, and hopefully he will teach it to others. I can't think of a cooler legacy, which brings up the question, "What passion or skill would *you* want to pass on to the next generation?"

I wanted to help students play guitar because several students told me they were uninspired or dropped out of their guitar class because it was too hard. Many students had purchased classical guitars because nylon strings were easier on their fingers compared to steel-string guitars. However, the problem is classical guitars have a wider nut width, and many of the students were females with small hands, making it extremely difficult for them to play and have fun. I wonder how many people quit guitar because they have an instrument that is not a proper fit for them. Or, as I previously touched upon, how many people quit because they are right-handed and they purchase a right-handed guitar, so they have to form chords with their non-dominant left hand? It's a shame because learning guitar is all about getting "over the hump." That is, beginners can start having fun if they can get to the point where they can transition between chords while maintaining tempo. In my experience, the vast majority of beginners never get to that point, thus missing out on a lifetime of joy and fulfillment.

CHAPTER SIXTEEN

HAPPINESS IS A BUTTERFLY

"Music is ... A higher revelation than all Wisdom and Philosophy."[1] Ludwig van Beethoven

AT THE BEGINNING of Joe Hagan's book, *Sticky Fingers: The Life and Times of Jann Wenner and Rolling Stone Magazine,* the author recounted the time Wenner drove John Lennon (his idol) and Yoko Ono around San Francisco. They drove by a movie theater and noticed that *A Hard Day's Night* was playing. Lennon had not seen it so they went inside.[2] As I read that story, I wondered what it would feel like to be in my early 20s driving around San Francisco with one of my idols in my car.

Fifty years later I worked at a university in California. Robert Plant (one of my rock 'n roll heroes) was scheduled to play a show on campus. When I left work on that day, I walked by his bus and someone came out. I asked the guy if Plant was around. He told me that Plant was going to fly in later that day. I considered hanging around for several hours to see if I could possibly meet Plant, because I knew where the entrances were to the venue where he was going to play. I decided not to stick around, but just the *thought* of possibly meeting Plant gave me a kick.

What is this fascination we have with celebrities? In my case, I saw the film *The Song Remains the Same* (a Led Zeppelin concert) on a large movie screen when I was an impressionable young man. I was so awestruck I had to go back the next day to see it again. They were like Gods on the big screen. I had a huge poster of Jimmy Page with his 12-string hanging in my bedroom, and I used to work up quite a sweat playing air-guitar to "Stairway to Heaven" and "Black Dog."

Growing up, my rock 'n roll heroes were Aynsley Dunbar and Neal Schon from Journey, Jimmy Page, Nancy Wilson, Ronnie Montrose, Tommy Bolin, and Tom Johnston (Springsteen would come later). I was mesmerized by Dunbar on the drums, and I wanted to be a drummer. Twenty years later, I discovered a used drum set in the basement of the school where I taught, so I started playing there on weekends. There was nobody around so I could play as long as I wanted. Later that year, two teachers and I decided to play a few songs for the graduating class on gradu-ation night. I was excited because now I was in a band! The other two teachers were musicians so they knew what they were doing. We played at a local restaurant and since this was before cell phones or the Internet, I have no idea how we sounded. Subsequently, I decided to purchase a drum set. I paid $2,000 and it had so many pieces Neil Peart himself would have been proud. The problem was I lived in a condominium and the neighbors complained, so I sold it to one of my seventh-grade students. He formed a band with his peers, which gave me immense satisfaction.

Thirty years later, the roles would be reversed when I retired from higher education. After 30 years in education (the last nine at a local university), I got a song. Several students performed an original song for me accompanied by three students on ukuleles. I can't imagine a better gift and I was extremely appreciative.

Someone asked me recently about my "bucket list." The top of my list would include meeting Bruce Springsteen in his home studio (I actually had a dream last night that I met him), as well as meeting Nancy Wilson, Jimmy Page, Tom Johnston, and Neal Schon. I discussed Springsteen's talents earlier. Nancy Wilson is the iconic female guitarist of my lifetime. Page is a legendary guitarist who has created more iconic riffs than any other rock guitarist, with the possible exception of Keith Richards. Johnston has written some of the greatest songs of all time. Schon is the lead guitarist for Journey, whose riffs have catapulted the band into superstar status. My bucket list also includes visiting Sicily and the Greek Islands, and going to the Masters Tournament in Augusta, Georgia. I'm not asking too much, am I?

And what would I say to Wilson, Springsteen, Page, Johnston, or Schon if I met them? I would ask them how much they play these days and if they have any new music about to be released. Also, since they're in their 60s or 70s, I would ask them if age h as any impact on their ability to play. I'm fascinated with this because at age 63 I feel like I'm fighting father time. Since I started playing at age 58, I haven't noticed any deterioration in my reflexes or skills, but that's probably because I didn't have skills to begin with. Hopefully I'm still in the improvement stage. I also would like to know if Page can still play his solo from "Black Dog" just like he did back in the day. Likewise, can Schon still pull off his scorching licks from "In the Morning Day?"

The phenomenon of celebrity is strange. I once stood in line at a movie theater behind the late San Francisco 49er Dwight Clark, who was responsible for my favorite sports memory (The Catch). I had my picture taken with Dwight Hicks and Carlton Williamson, also former 49ers. I congratulated Keena Turner (yes, another former 49er) in the locker room at my health club on his Super

Bowl win. Bjorn Borg (my boyhood tennis idol) walked past me at a tennis tournament. Greg Norman politely told me to step aside when I was in the way at Cypress Point Club. Jack Nicklaus walked by me during the 1987 U.S. Open at the Olympic Club. I rubbed elbows with several professional tennis players at the BNP Paribas Open tennis tournament in Indian Wells, including a conversation with Tommy Robredo at a local coffee shop where I suggested wheatgrass to maximize his health and recover from jet lag. He had never heard of it and thought I was nuts. I was thrilled when a friend took a picture of me with Willie Mays at the Crosby Clambake golf tournament, because he was my baseball idol when I was a kid. I met Jerry Rice during his rookie year in the NFL. I was in Big Brothers Big Sisters, and I had Rice sign a football for my "little brother." We played catch and Rice's signature wore off. How was I to know he would become of the greatest players of all time and his signature would become valuable?

I got a kick out of those moments, but it might be another matter if I met a rock 'n' roll legend. Why do I say this? Because the hair on my arms stood up when Tom Johnston and Patrick Simmons walked by me before a show in San Francisco. I mean, I was breathless. What a thrill. Moreover, thirty years ago I saw Paul Kantner (former guitarist for the Jefferson Airplane) in a parking lot in San Francisco and it gave me *chills*. He was a legend, part of the Haight-Ashbury scene in the late 60's. I also was happy when I received a reply on Facebook from Kevin Cadogan, who was the original guitarist on the first two Third Eye Blind albums. They are two of my favorite albums and his guitar work was extraordinary. He used different techniques and alternative tunings to make his guitar sound fuller, richer, and more exotic. After he left Third Eye Blind, he put out some strong solo albums, one of which was fantastic (*Thousand Yard Stare*).

MUSIC HAS SUCH a profound effect on us that we can experience an extreme sense of loss when rock 'n roll legends pass away. Some fans feel a deep connection with artists because their music has helped them through tough times, or perhaps they identify with particular lyrics. Additionally, music is part of our youth, so when legends pass away a part of our youth dies as well. But we'll always have the memories. It's a reminder that we are all mortal and our time is short, which is why it's important to do what we really want to do while we're still here.

As I write this, we've lost Kenny Rogers, Bill Withers, and John Prine during the last month, three legends whose staggering body of work is responsible for countless memories held by millions of fans. Some of the most beautiful and sentimental testimonials I've read are in the comments below their YouTube videos. Many fans are heartbroken and yet grateful for their music in the first place. Indeed, how lucky we are to be alive and hear the greatest music the world has ever produced. Consider the alternative, for all those whose lives ended before the 1960s, they never got to hear Marvin Gaye or Led Zeppelin or Jimi Hendrix or The Doors or Bruce Springsteen or the Beatles. It makes me wonder, when I am no longer physically on this planet, what incredible music will come out that I will never hear. But I'm okay with it because the music I've heard in my lifetime will keep me going for several lifetimes.

In particular, Tom Petty's death had a huge impact on me, as did Eddie Money and David Bowie. When Tom Petty passed away, it was as though a part of my foundation had crumbled because his music gave me so many great memories.

During my early 30s, my favorite band was Everything But The Girl, a British pop duo consisting of Ben Watt and Tracy Thorn. They wrote catchy and haunting pop songs like "Driving," "Understanding," "25th December," "Downtown Train," and "Miss You." These are some of the best songs I've heard and I couldn't get enough of this band. In 1992, Watt was hospitalized with Churg-Strauss syndrome, a rare life-threatening autoimmune disease. He lost a lot of weight and I was worried about him. Thankfully, he recovered, but I was surprised by how much I worried about someone I never met, which goes to show how important musicians are to the public.

My mom passed away in March 2019 from a two-year battle with cancer. It was stressful, and during that time I put my energy into guitar. It was a great release for me and gave me comfort. The one thing I could not do during that time was sing, because I didn't have it in my heart. Friends told me that I needed to sing during those trying times, but I couldn't bring myself to do it. I had no motivation to do so. After she passed, I felt like nothing mattered anymore, except playing guitar. I lost my motivation to do anything. All I wanted to do was play. It was my way of healing, and it helped me more than any words could. This is common for musicians, as several have told me they felt the same way at various points in their lives.

I wrote a song for my mom and tried to play it for her before she passed. She was sleepy from her medicine so she dozed off after a few seconds. On my mom's last day a couple of weeks later, my wife told me I should play my mom's song. She was unconscious but as soon as I hit the first chord she woke up and looked at me. She died later that day and I felt grateful that I was able to play her song for her. I haven't played the song since. I take heart in the fact that my mom told me she was proud of me for sticking with guitar. She said this because she knew better than anyone that I had a tendency to jump from one hobby to another.

My wife is from Hong Kong and is Buddhist. In her culture, people reappear as butterflies after they die. Sure enough, we saw two butterflies flying close together in our backyard after my mom died. At one point, they hovered a few feet above us. My wife said it was my mom and her late husband. Then, a few days later my wife found an old birthday card we had given her with a butterfly on the front. Later that day, my wife found a notebook of my mom's favorite proverbs. It turned out one of her favorite proverbs was about a butterfly: "Happiness is a butterfly, which, when pursued, is always just beyond your grasp, but which, if you will sit down quietly, may alight upon you."

This proverb was a stunning revelation to me because up until age 55 I was happiest when I played sports. Injuries forced me to stop. Now I have a hobby I enjoy while sitting down. I never imagined I could be happier sitting down than playing sports. This is why guitar can be so seductive. It puts me in a meditational state that can only be described as bliss.

My mom exhibited traits that I associate with a butterfly: Kind, beautiful, delicate, and blowing in the wind. For all of these reasons I decided to release my first song in her honor. The name of the song is "Butterfly Dance" and it's on YouTube. (This is not the song I wrote for her, as I haven't recorded it yet and don't know if I ever will. Rather, it's the first song I constructed digitally using prerecorded audio clips).

At the end of her life, I told my mom I wanted to write this book and send a letter to Springsteen. She got excited and said, "I think you should do that." She told me that 30 years earlier she had sent a letter to her favorite author Catherine Cookson, and received a reply. She thought it was a great idea to try to contact Springsteen, so I will. Thanks mom.

CHAPTER SEVENTEEN

THE LIGHTHOUSE

"Love is friendship set to music."[1] Jackson Pollock

ONE WAY MUSIC gets ingrained in our conscious is through films. When you think of the most powerful moments you've seen in movies, chances are many of them include music. For instance, consider how you felt when you heard the following:

- What a Feeling from *Flashdance*
- Purple Rain from *Purple Rain*
- Born to Be Wild from *Easy Rider*
- Eye of the Tiger from *Rocky III*
- Stayin' Alive from *Saturday Night Fever*
- Mrs. Robinson from *The Graduate*
- Raindrops Keep Falling on My Head from *Butch Cassidy and the Sundance Kid*
- In Your Eyes from *Say Anything*
- The Way We Were from *The Way We Were*
- Endless Love from *Endless Love*
- Streets of Philadelphia from *Philadelphia*

- Don't Cry for Me Argentina from *Evita*
- I Will Always Love You from *The Bodyguard*
- My Heart Will Go On from *Titanic*
- Theme songs from *Shaft, ET, Jaws, Star Wars, Chariots of Fire*

In addition, fans of animated films are well aware of the power of music in films like *Shrek, Frozen, Aladdin, Moana, Toy Story, Finding Nemo, Little Mermaid, Monsters, Inc., Despicable Me,* and *The Lion King*.

All of my favorite scenes from films include music. My favorite film is *Almost Famous* by Cameron Crowe. The soundtrack is outrageous but in particular my favorite scene is when Penny Lane (played by Kate Hudson) dances in an empty auditorium as Cat Stevens' "The Wind" plays in the background.[2] There is something profound and mesmerizing about that scene. The other scenes I like are the "Tiny Dancer" scene on the bus, as well as Led Zeppelin's "Tangerine" playing as the bus drives off into the distance at the end of the film.[2]

My favorite scenes from other films include the lunch scene from *My Best Friends' Wedding* when Rupert Everett breaks into "I Say a Little Prayer," the haunting music of Ennio Morricone in *Cinema Paradiso* during the outdoor cinema scene, several scenes from *School of Rock* with Jack Black, and the last scene from *Love Actually* set to the music of the Beach Boys' "God Only Knows." I also like the scene in *Once,* where Glen Hansard and his female companion jam in a music store. And even though it wasn't in a film, I can't leave out one of my favorite scenes from television. It took place in *Freaks and Geeks* (the greatest show ever about what it's like to be in high school) when actor Jason Segel channeled Rush drummer Neil Peart. It was a dream scene for any adolescent male who fantasized about being a rock star.

Finally, there's the last scene with Robert Redford and Barbra Streisand from *The Way We Were,* as well as *The Unbearable Light-*

ness of Being soundtrack, especially the moving piano piece as the film ends.

In terms of favorite scenes from musicals, documentaries, or concert films, the list is too long to go into. In these types of films, music is expected, compared to "traditional" films where music can hit you unexpectedly. This can leave a lasting imprint because of the emotions facilitated by the combination of the music and the content of the film itself. I like to be surprised by the songs filmmakers choose to include in their films.

There's one film scene that takes on added importance. It's the scene from *Moulin Rouge* where Ewan McGregor sings Elton John's "Your Song" to Nicole Kidman. It's absolute magic, especially the second half of the song when they are on the rooftops. When I watched that scene, I thought it would be special if I could sing that song to my girlfriend.

Two years later, I wanted to surprise her with my marriage proposal, so I booked a helicopter tour to a lighthouse located a few miles off the coast of California. I set it up so the tour director would give me two minutes alone to propose at the top of the lighthouse. My fantasy was to sing "Your Song" to her before getting down on one knee. It turned out to be nothing more than a dream because I had never sung before and I didn't get around to signing up for singing lessons. It's just as well because of what occurred on the day of the proposal.

Once we arrived at the airport, there was an hour delay due to heavy fog, which was so dense we couldn't even see the water. The thought of flying in dense fog so close to the water without being able to see the water was a little scary, but at the same time I thought it would be a great surprise for my girlfriend because she wouldn't know we were over water and then minutes later we would land on a lighthouse, the last place in the world anyone would expect to land. Since we had an hour delay, we decided to walk down to the beach. I was extremely nervous. My body was shaking and I became emotional because

I was 47 years old and I'd never been married, so I understood the magnitude of the situation. I couldn't wait any longer so I got down on one knee and proposed. We never took the helicopter ride. But it's the thought that counts?

One question I've asked myself for decades is, "If I made a film, which song would I choose to open the film?" Would I choose haunting music similar to the opening of films like *The Piano, Apocalypse Now,* or *The Big Blue*? The opening songs of those films sucked me right in. Perhaps a scorching solo from Jimi Hendrix, David Gilmour, or Stevie Ray Vaughn? That's a good way to get the audience's blood pumping. Pink Floyd's "Time" or "Money" could also set the stage for a film. Perhaps something from the Zeppelin catalog? How about "Born to Run," the quintessential American rock song and in my humble opinion the greatest rock song by an American band? What about "Girl Crush" from Little Big Town? "Avalon" from Roxy Music? Motown? There are hundreds of songs by Motown artists that would be worthy candidates. Or perhaps John Coltrane's "Welcome?" I haven't heard a more beautiful song than that one. The same goes for several songs by Enya. Or maybe Frank Sinatra's nostalgic "It Was a Very Good Year?" On the other end of the spectrum, what about "Love Stinks" by The J. Geils Band? That would be an appropriate song if the film was about the end of a relationship. Or perhaps an electronic anthem like "Time to Pretend," the opening song from *21*? I couldn't wait to get my hands on that song. As far as the content of the film itself, it reminded me of my college days when I counted cards to win at blackjack. The first time I counted cards I made $120, but it took all night to do it since I was betting only two dollars a hand.

If my real life could mirror any character I've seen on the big screen, it would be William Miller in *Almost Famous,* the high school journalism student who writes for *Rolling Stone Magazine* while he tours the country with the band Stillwater.[2] Heck, I was excited from simply watching bands in concert when I was in high school; the thought of actually getting to tour with a band? What a dream.

Question: Are songs in films more popular than they would be if they weren't in films? After all, there's a strong association between what's happening on the screen and the music itself that allows us to form connections. How many times have we heard songs that take us back to film scenes? This explains why so many favorite scenes include music.

I HAVE a theory that there are some songs very few people dislike. I think "Hey Soul Sister" is one of them. Along those lines, it would be interesting to find out the percentage of people who like any particular song. In other words, what percentage of people polled would like "Hey Soul Sister," versus percentages for other songs? I assume there has never been a song that 100% of the public likes, but what would be the most popular songs according to this metric?

Given that each song speaks to us in its own way and we attach meaning to songs depending on the sum of our life experience, what is the most appropriate metric to rate the popularity of songs? In our culture we use sales or the number of views online, but that doesn't include those who are marginalized, can't afford to buy music, do not have Internet access, or have lost interest in purchasing music. In order to quantify the most popular songs, should we use sales, royalties, polls, number of views online, or number of weeks on the charts? The top songs vary according to the criteria we use.

For instance, if the criterion is best-selling physical singles, the top songs are:

- Bing Crosby: White Christmas"[3]
- Elton John: Candle in the Wind[3]
- Mungo Jerry: In The Summertime[4][5][6]
- Bing Crosby: Silent Night[7]
- Bill Haley and His Comets: Rock Around the Clock[8]

If we wanted to find the most popular songs guitar players want to play, the list would look different. We could use ultimate-guitar.com. The top songs are:[9]

- Jeff Buckley: Hallelujah
- John Legend: All of Me
- Passenger: Let Her Go
- Ed Sheeran: Perfect
- Led Zeppelin: Stairway to Heaven

If the criterion is number of views on YouTube, we get a completely different list:[10]

- Luis Fonsi: (feat. Daddy Yankee) Despacito
- Ed Sheeran: Shape of You
- Wiz Khalifa: (feat. Charlie Puth) See You Again
- Mark Ronson: (feat. Bruno Mars) Uptown Funk
- PSY: Gangham Style

If the criterion is royalties, the top songs (as of Feb 2017) are:[11]

- White Christmas by Irving Berlin
- You've Lost that Lovin' Feeling by B. Mann, C. Weil & P. Spector
- Yesterday by Paul McCartney (credited as Lennon/McCartney)
- Unchained Melody by Alex North & Hy Zaret

- Stand By Me by Ben E King, Jerry Leiber, and Mike Stoller

There are several options if we use the length of time on the Billboard charts. Do we judge songs by length of time in the Top 100, the Top 10, or at Number One? A defining hallmark of a great song is its sustainability; that is, how long it remains relevant with the listening public. For this reason, let's use the number of weeks in the Top 100 as our criterion. If so, the top songs are:[12]

- Radioactive: Imagine Dragons
- Awolnation: Sail
- Jason Marz: I'm Yours
- LeAnn Rimes: How Do I Live

In 2012, *Rolling Stone Magazine* published their list of the 500 Greatest Songs of All Time, stemming from a poll of critics, industry figures, and rock musicians. If we use this list as the criterion, the top songs are:[13]

- Bob Dylan: Like a Rolling Stone
- The Rolling Stones: I Can't Get No Satisfaction
- John Lennon: Imagine
- Marvin Gaye: What's Going On
- Aretha Franklin: Respect

Amazingly, 94% of the 500 greatest songs are by artists from the US and the UK (England, Scotland, Wales, and Northern Ireland).[13] However, this is not surprising given that rock 'n roll was born out of the blues in the US and then spread across the pond to the UK. Consequently, guitarists who were part of the so-called "British Invasion" were influenced by blues' guitarists, some of which included Chuck Berry, Little Richard,

John Lee Hooker, Freddie King, Robert Johnson, Louis Jordan, T-Bone Walker, BB King, Muddy Waters, Bessie Smith, Willie Dixon, Sonny Boy Williamson, Buddy Guy, Howling Wolf, Buddy King, Otis Rush, and Little Walton.

Take a look at the chart below. What do all of these guitar players have in common?

- Jimmy Page
- Keith Richards
- David Gilmour
- Eric Clapton
- John Lennon
- George Harrison
- Brian May
- Ronnie Wood
- Pete Townsend
- The Edge
- Peter Frampton
- Jeff Beck
- Peter Green
- Ritchie Blackmore
- Paul McCartney
- Robin Trower
- David Cloverdale
- Angus Young
- Malcolm Young
- Mick Ronson
- The Great Kat
- Jeff Lynne
- Hank Marvin
- Steve Howe
- Chris Squire
- Mike Rutherford
- Tony Iommi

- John McLaughlin
- Brian Jones
- Greg Lake
- Alvin Lee
- Dave Mason
- Mick Taylor
- Robert Fripp
- Mark Knopfler
- Slash
- Steve Marriott
- Brian Jones
- Gary Moore
- Jimi Hendrix
- Stevie R. Vaughn
- BB King
- Steve Vai
- Prince
- Danny Gatton
- Albert King
- Mike Bloomfield
- Tom Morello
- Kirk Hammett
- Joe Satriani
- Lita Ford
- John Mayer
- John Petrucci
- Billie Gibbons
- Dave Mustaine
- Zakk Wylde
- Chuck Berry
- Frank Zappa
- Lou Reed
- Nancy Wilson
- Joan Jett

- James Hatfield
- Billie Joe Armstrong
- Jerry Garcia
- Jack White
- Joe Perry
- Duane Allman
- Bruce Springsteen
- Joe Walsh
- Carlos Santana
- Eric Johnson
- Buddy Guy
- Les Paul
- Neil Young
- Stephen Stills
- Trey Anastasio
- Johnny Winter
- Lindsey Buckingham
- Chet Atkins
- Bo Diddly
- Bob Weir
- Glen Campbell
- Leslie West
- Joe Bonomassa
- Brad Paisley
- Gary Rossington
- John Mayall
- Dickie Betts

Answer: All of the guitar players on this list were born in the US or the UK. That's right, the overwhelming majority of the greatest guitar players in rock 'n roll come from the same four countries that produced 94% of the 500 Greatest Songs of All Time. A coincidence?

The following is a breakdown of the percentage of songs on

the list represented by each decade. Notice that more than 65% of the songs come from the 1960s and 1970s.[13]

- 1940s 2%
- 1950s 13.6%
- 1960s 39.2%
- 1970s 26.2%
- 1980s 11%
- 1990s 4.4%
- 2000s 5.4%

Again, what is the most appropriate metric to rate the popularity of songs? After all, "Happy Birthday" has probably been sung the most and had the greatest positive effect on the largest number of people. In fact, "Happy Birthday" used to earn the highest royalties, but no longer receives royalties because it's now in the public domain.[14] Similarly, Christmas carols are probably in the upper echelon of songs that have the greatest positive impact on people, given their proclivity for lifting the human spirit. Religious hymns or chants are in the same category.

My guess is most people would say their favorite songs are those that make them feel most alive and happy (although to be fair many of us also like songs that make us sad). So, where in life do we combine music with feeling most alive and happy? The answer is when we sing or dance, whether in drum circles, in nightclubs, at weddings, at concerts, or alone in our bedroom. There's a catharsis that occurs when we let go to sing or dance. For many people, dancing evokes some of the best memories of their lives, and if you remember having a great time dancing at some point in your life, chances are you might remember the music that was playing.

While on the topic of dancing, I was a sales representative for a toy company when I was a young man. My territory included the Western United States, so I traveled extensively. I used to listen to my Walkman and dance in my hotel room, often practicing Michael Jackson's moonwalk. I must've been out of my mind and looked ridiculous but that's what naïve 25-year-old males do sometimes. Some of the songs I used to dance to included KC and the Sunshine Band's "Give It Up," Cheryl Lynn's "Got to Be Real," the Emotions' "Best of My Love," and The J. Geils' Band "Give It To Me." The last minute and a half of the latter song is among the funkiest I've ever heard.

CHAPTER EIGHTEEN

THE CLASSICS

"Softly, deftly, music shall caress you. Hear it, feel it, secretly possess you."[1] Charles Hart

MANY FROM MY generation believe the quality of music has gone downhill. Where are the classic albums of today? Of course, we won't know what is considered classic until many years from now.

I can still find great songs here and there but it's nothing like when I was a teenager. Of course, decreasing dopamine levels probably has something to do with that. Nevertheless, out of curiosity I decided to list some of the greatest albums from 1965-1975, which takes me through my high school years. Remember that 65% of *Rolling Stone Magazine's* 500 Greatest Songs of All Time were from the 1960s and 1970s? Look no further than the list below for confirmation. This is a stunning list full of legendary and influential albums that defined rock 'n roll in its heyday. Personally, a case could be made that the seminal albums released in 1975, 1973, and 1971 *alone* could stack up against all the legendary albums released since then.

The list:

1975

- Fleetwood Mac (*Fleetwood Mac*)
- KISS (*Alive*)
- Alice Cooper (*Welcome to My Nightmare*)
- Bruce Springsteen (*Born to Run*)
- Journey (*Journey*)
- Eagles (*One of These Nights*)
- Heart (*Dreamboat Annie*)
- Led Zeppelin (*Physical Graffiti*)
- Aerosmith (*Toys in the Attic*)
- Jeff Beck (*Blow By Blow*)
- Electric Light Orchestra (*Face the Music*)
- Pink Floyd (*Wish You Were Here*)
- Queen (*A Night at the Opera*)
- Paul Simon (*Still Crazy after All These Years*)
- Bob Dylan (*Blood on the Tracks*)
- ABBA (*ABBA*)

1974

- Bad Company (*Bad Company*)
- Lou Reed (*Rock 'n Roll Animal*)
- Eric Clapton (*461 Ocean Boulevard*)
- Robin Trower (*Bridges of Sighs*)
- David Bowie (*Diamond Dogs*)
- Joni Mitchell (*Court and Spark*)
- Queen (*Sheer Heart Attack*)
- Queen (*Queen II*)
- KISS (*KISS*)

1973

- The Who (*Quadrophenia*)
- Elton John (*Goodbye Yellow Brick Road*)
- Paul McCartney and Wings (*Band on the Run*)
- Lynyrd Skynyrd (*Lynyrd Skynyrd*)
- Bruce Springsteen (*The Wild, the Innocent and the E St. Shuffle; Greetings from Ashbury Park*)
- The Doobie Brothers (*The Captain and Me*)
- Emerson Lake and Palmer (*Brain Salad Surgery*)
- New York Dolls (*New York Dolls*)
- Pink Floyd (*Dark Side of the Moon*)
- Stevie Wonder (*Interventions*)
- Led Zeppelin (*Houses of the Holy*)
- Aerosmith (*Aerosmith*)
- Montrose (*Montrose*)

1972

- Neil Young (*Harvest*)
- Jim Croce (*You Don't Mess Around with Jim*)
- Todd Rundgren (*Something Anything*)
- Steely Dan (*Can't Buy a Thrill*)
- David Bowie (*The Rise and Fall of Ziggy Stardust and the Spiders from Mars*)
- Deep Purple (*Machine Head*)
- The Rolling Stones (*Exile on Main Street*)
- Stevie Wonder (*Talking Book*)

1971

- Joni Mitchell (*Blue*)
- The Doors (*LA Woman*)
- Yes (*Fragile; The Yes Album*)
- Rod Stewart (*Every Picture Tells a Story*)
- Janis Joplin (*Pearl*)

- Cat Stevens (*Teaser and the Firecat*)
- The Who (*Who's Next)*
- Led Zeppelin (*Led Zeppelin VI)*
- Marvin Gaye (*What's Going On*)
- The Rolling Stones (*Sticky Fingers*)
- Carole King (*Tapestry*)
- Jethro Tull (*Aqualung*)

1970

- Creedence Clearwater Revival (*Cosmo's Factory*)
- Led Zeppelin (*Led Zeppelin III*)
- Van Morrison (*Moondance*)
- Miles Davis (*Bitches Brew*)
- George Harrison (*All Things Must Pass*)
- Neil Young (*After the Gold Rush*)
- Black Sabbath (*Paranoid*)
- Beatles (*Let It Be*)
- Crosby Stills Nash and Young (*Déjà Vu*)
- Cat Stevens (*Tea for the Tillerman*)
- Derek and the Dominoes (*Layla and Other Assorted Love Songs*)
- Santana (*Abraxas*)
- The Who (*Live at Leeds*)
- Elton John (*Tumbleweed Connection*)
- James Taylor (*Sweet Baby James*)
- Joni Mitchell (*Ladies of the Canyon*)

1969

- The Rolling Stones (*Let It Bleed*)
- Creedence Clearwater Revival (*Willie and the Poor Boys; Bayou Country*)
- Neil Young and Crazy Horse (*Everybody Knows This Is*

Nowhere)
- Joni Mitchell (*Clouds*)
- Stevie Wonder (*My Cherie Amour*)
- Beatles (*Abbey Road; Yellow Submarine*)
- Led Zeppelin (*Led Zeppelin; Led Zeppelin II*)
- The Who (*Tommy*)
- David Bowie (*Space Odyssey*)

1968

- Beatles (*The White Album*)
- Velvet Underground (*White Light White Heat*)
- Simon and Garfunkel (*Bookends*)
- The Rolling Stones (*Beggars Banquet*)
- Van Morrison (*Astral Weeks*)
- The Jimi Hendrix Experience (*Electric Lady Land*)
- Aretha Franklin (*Lady Soul*)
- Blood, Sweat & Tears (*Blood, Sweat & Tears*)

1967

- Beatles (*Magical Mystery Tour; Sgt. Pepper's Lonely Hearts Club Band*)
- The Jimi Hendrix Experience (*Are You Experienced; Axis: Bold As Love*)
- The Doors (*The Doors*)

1966

- Beatles (*Revolver*)
- Beach Boys (*Pet Sounds*)
- The Mamas and the Papas (*If You Can Believe Your Eyes and Ears*)

- Simon and Garfunkel (*Parsley, Sage, Rosemary and Thyme*)
- John Mayall and Eric Clapton (*Blues Breakers*)

1965

- Beach Boys (*Summer Days (and Summer Nights!!)*
- Beatles (*Help; Rubber Soul*)
- The Who (*My Generation*)
- Bob Dylan (*Highway 61 Revisited*)

Given the quality and quantity of these legendary albums, it's hard to question that 1965-1975 represented the best span of rock 'n roll music. Since the public can now purchase individual songs instead of albums, it seems like there isn't enough inertia for the public to build consensus or get behind revolutionary albums that might be considered classic in the future.

CHAPTER NINETEEN

SELFIES, COOKIES, AND GIFT BAGS

"People haven't always been there for me but music always has."[1] Taylor Swift

I RECENTLY WATCHED a Netflix documentary on Taylor Swift. It was fascinating to see her creative process, especially the way she creates lyrics and melody.

Playing guitar has given me a newfound appreciation for musicians and songwriters. They deserve the utmost respect, yet some critical reviews are far too harsh. I understand if people don't care for someone's music, but to bash an artist for personal reasons is shameful and toxic. Some people criticize Swift for one thing or another and yet they don't know her at all. On top of that, many have never played an instrument and have no idea how to write a song.

There's a video on YouTube that explains why Swift is a better guitar player than she is given credit for. The contention is that she's always in rhythm and plays to her vocals, among other strengths.[2] I have no idea how competent of a guitar player she is but I do know that she is the complete package.

You don't sell more than 75 million singles and be the best-selling female artist of the last decade without good reason.[3] She is an astonishing songwriter who writes songs that connect with hundreds of millions of listeners. That is not easy to do. And let's not forget the amount of work she put in for years before she hit it big. It takes courage to put music out in the world and she started doing it at a young age. The other thing I respect about her is that she has remained grounded, even after receiving so many platitudes at such a young age.

I used to give presentations for my fantasy sports programs to teachers throughout the country. I was surprised at how many people told me I was a genius or I was brilliant. Some wanted me to sign my books. It was uncomfortable because I knew I was just a guy from a small town who happened to like math, writing, and fantasy sports, and somehow forces in the universe aligned for me to combine those interests. I was uncomfortable receiving so much praise and there were times when I asked myself if I deserved the attention. It wasn't always easy to stay grounded when so many people were telling me how great I was. And I was 50 years old when this happened. Consequently, I can understand why some young celebrities can't handle fame. It's overwhelming. They don't know who they are yet. But Swift seems to have figured out how to deal with it. I'm not saying it was easy but from my perspective on the outside it seems as though she has handled fame better than some of her contemporaries.

Swift also doesn't forget her fans. She has been known to invite them to her home where she plays her latest release for them. She spends time with each individual fan taking selfies. She also bakes cookies for them and gives them gift bags.[4] Can you think of any other artist who does anything like that? Not only that, but she stood up for artists when she went up against Apple a few years back, which garnered her respect from her peers. To all her critics, it's time to let go and give her a break.

CHAPTER TWENTY

EATING PANCAKES TO JUMPIN' JACK FLASH

"The universe is making music all the time"[1] Tom Waits

IN FULL DISCLOSURE, music lovers may not like what I'm about to say. Namely, the only time I don't care for music is when it's forced on me, usually in a restaurant, shopping mall, grocery store, or at a sporting event. I'm referring to loud "background" music. Eating Swedish pancakes for breakfast while "Jumpin' Jack Flash" is blasting away is not my idea of a pleasant meal. I like to eat in silence and read if I'm by myself, or engage in conversation if I'm with someone. Likewise, "Smoke on the Water" does not tempt me to buy more groceries.

These examples pale in comparison to the volume of music at sporting events, which is why I stopped going to professional, college, and high school basketball games. Whenever there was a break in the action, the music would take over. I couldn't have a conversation with the person sitting next to me unless I raised my voice considerably and leaned in so he could hear. The joy of talking about the game was eliminated. I realize venues try to create a high-energy atmosphere, and I can understand loud music before games because it might help motivate players. However, there is no need to inundate fans with loud music during timeouts. Furthermore, the last time I went to a professional basketball game, the music often played while the game was in session.

Music in public areas permeates our lives. I'm amazed at the number of businesses that play loud music. When I asked an employee at a restaurant to turn the volume down, he looked at me like I was crazy. Evidently, the customer is not always right.

Does background music really lead to a more pleasant shopping experience? At a time when we are bombarded with music seemingly everywhere we go, have we reached the point of saturation? Indeed, has anyone ever complained because of a *lack* of background music? Are there actual studies that prove a direct correlation between sales and background music at Everystore, USA? Apparently, decreasing the volume – or turning off the music all together - will result in customers fleeing in droves. Contrary to popular opinion, silence is not golden after all.

Noise pollution is ubiquitous in our culture, whether from airplanes, stereos, televisions, construction, traffic, or sporting events. Any sustained sound at 70 dB or higher can lead to ear damage, and any sound at 120 dB or higher can immediately damage the inner workings of the ear.[2] With this in mind, I would like to see results of large-scale studies on employees' loss of hearing at video arcades in shopping malls.

Enter the younger generation, who cannot live without their earbuds, earphones, or in-ear headphones. Consider how many hours a day adolescents listen to music on their portable music players. Consequently, it's not surprising that a three-year study of 3,316 children aged nine to eleven found a prevalence of high-frequency hearing loss of 14.2%. This hearing loss was associated with headphone use, used by 40% of the cohort.[3]

I used to belong to a health club that played the same loud

music every afternoon, even though there were 40 different stations available. Complaints went unheeded, as the manager informed me that, "People like to work out to loud, fast music." A quick survey found there were only four people in the club at that time, all senior citizens. No one enjoyed the music and some preferred not having any music at all, as those of us in our later years enjoy the personal insights that often come with silence. After all, isn't the point of exercise to get in touch with one's body? Truly, the older I get, the more I treasure silence. When I want to listen to music, I want to *listen* to music. But that's just me.

CHAPTER TWENTY-ONE

WHAT'S NEXT

"The only truth is music."[1] Jack Kerouac

I'D LIKE to get to the point where I'm comfortable playing and singing in front of an audience. The only way to do that is to play and sing in front of an audience. When I began playing, I thought I would play at a local coffee house within six months. Here I am, five years later. I am getting more comfortable playing in front of one person. It comes down to a lack of confidence in my singing voice. Unfortunately, confidence is everything. Even singers who don't have great voices sound fine because they have confidence.

The ultimate dream is to be in a band. In 2019, I visited my dentist and started talking to his dental assistant. She played bass and her husband played lead guitar. I told her I played rhythm and the drums a little bit. She was interested in all of us getting together. When I drove home that day, I was excited at the prospect of being in a band, even though I knew I wasn't good enough yet. But hey, why let something like that get in the way? She told me she was also a singer and some of her friends told her she sounded like the singer from Mazzy Star. I hadn't listened to Mazzy Star for years but I did remember their singer had a unique voice. Visions of headlining at the local taco house were swirling in my head. She called me one day and said she would call me when they got back from a short road trip. I never heard from her again.

I'd like to learn some solos. However, it's time-consuming. I spent a month trying to learn the solo to Eddie Money's "Two Tickets to Paradise" and I only learned the first three bars or so. So even though I want to learn solos, I guess I'd rather put the time into learning new songs so I see more of an immediate payback. My favorite solos include The Doobie Brothers' "Without You," Prince's "Purple Rain," The Marshall Tucker Band's "Green Grass and High Tides," Led Zeppelin's "Black Dog," Bon Jovi's "Wanted Dead or Alive," The Isley Brothers' "Who's That Lady," Pink Floyd's "Comfortably Numb," and Alvin Lee's "I'd Love to Change the World."

In addition, I'd like to master the songs on my setlist, as well as iconic licks like "I'm Coming Out" by Diana Ross, "Fire on High" by Electric Light Orchestra, and the end of "What Is and What Never Should Be" by Led Zeppelin. The latter was Jimmy Page at his best. He was a master at using space and patterns to create rhythm. I actually learned this riff a couple of years ago but it was too difficult because I couldn't turn my wrist enough to play in the upper frets and I kept hitting dead notes. I was able to play it a little bit but I let it go after practicing it every day for a month. It has escaped my memory until now so I will try again.

I'd also like to get to the point where I can play a B major chord in the second and fourth frets, even though I can't spread my first and third fingers out enough to do so. But that's not going to stop me from trying. I'm improving, although not as quickly as I would like. I think it's safe to assume that every guitar player would like to progress quicker than they do because there is much to learn.

Additionally, I want to visit Norman's Rare Guitars in Southern California, a renowned store. They've posted several videos of professionals playing in their store. My favorite segment is "The Greatest Moments from Norman's Rare Guitars Part One," where the late Alvin Lee plays an acoustic at 11:00 followed by four guys trading off licks to Average White Band's "Work to Do."[2] It's funky and hot. I would love to be able to play that riff but I'm not physically able to play the barre chords. I tried substitute chord shapes but it didn't sound the same. The video also includes Don McLean, Richie Sambora, Orianthi, and several other professionals trying out guitars and jamming.

I'd also like to take a self-guided tour of famous rock venues, recording studios, and homes where rock 'n roll legends lived in San Francisco during the Summer of Love.[3] I want to see where Janis Joplin, Jimi Hendrix, the Grateful Dead, and the Jefferson Airplane lived. That would be a treat for me because I used to live in the San Francisco Bay Area.

Perhaps most important, I want to learn music theory. I signed up for an online course so now I don't have any excuses. I've dabbled in theory a little bit, but I've heard too many professionals say that music theory opened up a new world for them on the fretboard. I'm looking forward to it.

My primary focus when I finish this book is to record my original songs. I haven't discussed them because I haven't recorded them yet and consequently they are not in the public domain. I need to fine-tune them, create better hooks, and explore different progressions and melodies. Like any beginner singer-songwriter, I have a lot to learn. That said, I believe one of my songs could be a major hit with the right singer. The chorus is a monster, the lyrics are catchy and memorable, and the song is hot. But how do I get distribution if I can't even sing it good enough to record a decent-sounding demo?

Like I stated earlier in the book, I need to either find a guitar with more projection or figure out how to increase the sound on my guitar during my recordings. Once I record my songs, I'd like to sell them to a music publisher or get selected for *Songland*. Of course this is all a pie-in-the-sky fantasy because I am no more ready to go on *Songland* than I am to pull off a Hendrix solo. But it doesn't hurt to put it out there. It's all about the journey, right? Perhaps the universe will meet me halfway. People might think I'm nuts, but even an old man can dream. That said, the rate of success in the music industry is astronomically low. In order to get a hit record, first I need to write a great song, then get it recorded, then market it on social media, then land a recording contract, then write and record several additional songs to complete an album, all of this while playing hundreds of gigs in the meantime. It doesn't happen overnight. And how much of a role does serendipity play? For instance, when Tom Petty first arrived in Los Angeles as a young man, he went inside a phone booth to start calling record companies. He picked up a piece of paper on the ground and it turned out to be a list of 25 record labels with their numbers and addresses. Within three days he had interest from three labels.[4] Would that have occurred without picking up that piece of paper? That is the question. Does the cream always rise to the top in the music industry, resulting in a recording contract? There have been plenty of brilliant artists who could not get published for one reason or another. How many talented artists work hard for decades only to never make it? Is it bad luck? Or do we make our own destiny? Does hard work and persistence *always* pay off?

We live in an age where talent doesn't always win. There are plenty of musicians who have managed to carve a niche in the music industry via their presence on social media, where they have generated enough interest from fans to make a difference. Often, adolescents respond to young artists who project a certain lifestyle: They look cool, dress cool, act cool, and project attitude. To some adolescents, these traits may be more important than the quality of the music itself.

For those who are fortunate enough to land a music publisher, there's a standard industry-average royalty. For instance, if a publisher was interested in one of my songs, they would pitch it to their artists. If an artist decided to include it on their album, then I would earn royalties. There are three main types of royalties: performance royalties from radio, synchronize royalties (licensing to films, television, or advertisements), and mechanical royalties from album sales and digital downloads.

There are several sources for royalties, including hotels, restaurants, shopping malls, and professional sports franchises. In terms of royalties from films or television, producers often use only a few seconds of a song. The songs I constructed digitally from audio clips are mashups, so there are several different sections in each song that could be possibilities. I realize this is a pipedream, but who knows?

Some artists are so protective of their music that they do not allow tutorials of their songs on YouTube or allow chords or lyrics for their songs to be posted on sites like ultimate-guitar.com. If artists want to maximize their brand, doesn't it make sense to want as many people as possible learning to play their songs, thereby maximizing exposure? After all, we live in a world of impressions, the more the better. Some musicians who post covers on YouTube get thousands, if not millions, of views, which is additional exposure for original artists. Some listeners who hear cover songs might like them and may want to buy the original. Consequently, professional musicians might be hurting themselves financially when they don't let amateurs cover their songs. In an industry where imitation is the sincerest form of flattery, I would think professional artists would enjoy the thought of other artists covering their songs, up to a point.

That said, I can understand where artists are coming from.

First, I can identify with copyright infringement because I had several people plagiarize parts of my books. Second, some musicians are financially independent and don't need additional exposure. Third, many musicians do not get into the music industry for money. The music itself is what's most important to them, so the thought of artists covering their songs might bother them and supersede any potential benefits from additional exposure. Finally, if I was a professional musician, I don't think I would enjoy hearing terrible covers of my songs. I wouldn't want the integrity of the songs to be undermined.

CHAPTER TWENTY-TWO

EARWORMS

"If music be the food of love, play on."[1] William Shakespeare

HAVE you ever listened to an empowering song and wanted to become someone else, or suddenly believed you could conquer the world? If so, at what point during the song did those feelings arise? Chances are you felt this way during the chorus because it usually contains the highest emotional energy in a song. Choruses are what listeners wait for and remember best. The first chorus in a song almost always occurs before the one-minute mark and the "hook" leaves a lasting impression. This is not to denigrate verses, because they contain the most meaningful lyrics and generate emotional energy so the chorus can then explode.

Choruses are usually the favorite part of songs because they inspire us and make us feel good. Even if listeners can't recall lyrics in verses, they can often remember lyrics in choruses. Choruses can be empowering and make us feel as though we can be anybody and do anything. That is the magic of music.

I look forward to choruses because they connect with me on

some level. They can become so ingrained in my subconscious that I can't get them out of my head. These "earworms" (i.e., a song or short piece of music that stays in your head) are common and can be voluntary or involuntary. One poll found that 90% of the population has an earworm once a week. However, it's not always a pleasant experience, as 15% of listeners said their earworm was "disturbing."[2]

On the other hand, I have a friend who has an earworm every morning when she wakes up. Amazingly, the earworm plays into something she learns that day. It's as though her subconscious provides clues as to what's going to take place that day. I also often have earworms when I wake up. If there's one band that gives me more earworms than any other, it's Coldplay. Their sound takes me past the stratosphere into the ionosphere. I can't think of another band in this millennium that has so many iconic riffs. In my humble opinion, I believe they have been one of the greatest bands in the world since their debut album in 2000. But that's just my two cents.

One study found that the possibility of a song becoming an earworm can be predicted based on melody, tempo, how recent the song is, and the popularity of the song.[3] According to 3,000 participants in the study, the top earworms were:[3]

- Bad Romance by Lady Gaga
- Can't Get You Out Of My Head by Kylie Minogue
- Don't Stop Believing by Journey
- Somebody That I Used To Know by Gotye
- Moves Like Jagger by Maroon 5

Similar to reading a book, studies indicate that listeners continually generate expectations of what will occur next in a song. One study found that the pleasure derived from music was based on listener expectations and whether or not those expectations were met.[4] Pleasure was derived when listeners anticipated a certain sound and were surprised when the sound was different from what they expected. For instance, the pitch of the singer's voice was higher or lower than what was expected, or perhaps there was a significant change in chords or notes. The highest pleasure was derived when listeners were most surprised because they incorrectly predicted what was coming next.[4] This is interesting because in the aforementioned list of the top earworms, Lady Gaga not only had the top earworm, she also had two more earworms in the top 10 as well. The question is, what is she doing that connects so much with the listening public? My guess is it has to do with the combination of her pitch and chord changes in her songs. They often are completely unexpected.

Many of my earworms are intros or outros. In fact, the only disappointment I feel when I listen to music is that some songs end too soon. The outro can be the best part of the song and I wish that the artist had incorporated it into the song earlier. Sometimes the song ends with a solo and it's either cut off or fades out. For instance, "Driving" (Everything But The Girl) fades away as a sax solo begins. I wish I could hear more of that solo. Likewise, the outro in "Natural Thing" (The Doobie Brothers) is so melodic and smooth, I wish it would last longer. But no complaints, we are lucky to have great songs like this in the first place.

Another study aimed to find the catchiest songs of all time by timing how quickly 12,000 listeners could recognize songs. The top songs were:[5]

- Spice Girls: Wannabe - 2.29 s (0:45)
- Lou Bega: Mambo No. 5 - 2.48 s (0:50)
- Survivor: Eye of the Tiger - 2.62 s (2:04)
- Lady Gaga: Just Dance - 2.66 s (1:39)
- ABBA: SOS - 2.73 s (2:25)

Choruses bring joy to our lives. One such chorus for me is from "Drift Away" by Dobie Gray. Due to copyright issues I cannot include the lyrics here, but I don't believe there has ever been better lyrics for a chorus in any song. Another chorus that sticks with me is from "Hey Soul Sister" by Train. It's a mesmerizing chorus with great lyrics and rhythm. Then there's "Two Tickets to Paradise" by Eddie Money, one of the greatest choruses ever written. It's powerful and easy to remember. Other examples include "Listen to the Music" by The Doobie Brothers, "You Ain't Seen Nothing Yet" by Bachman-Turner Overdrive, "We're an American Band" by Grand Funk Railroad, "School's Out for Summer" by Alice Cooper, and "Bennie and the Jets" by Elton John.

Some songs don't have a chorus. For instance, Queen's "Bohemian Rhapsody" was a monster hit without the use of a chorus. Moreover, some of the most powerful choruses don't include words. Instead, short, repetitive sounds like oh, da, na, or ba are used. This can be extremely effective. One example is "Hey Jude."

Sometimes a song turns into a national celebration, and when that song has one of the best hooks ever produced, it can create its own ethos. For instance, consider "Call Me Maybe" by Carly Rae Jepsen. It became a sensation when it was released in 2012. Teachers, construction workers, hospital staff, and countless employees from other occupations created their own covers of the song. People of all ages and from all walks of life joined in on the fun. It became a national sensation. As of this writing, the song has 1.27 billion views on YouTube with only 327,000 thumbs-down, which means that only .0257% did not like the song.[6] In other words, for every 3,895 listeners who watched the video, only one person gave it a thumbs down. I don't know the average percentage of thumbs-down on YouTube videos, but that is extremely low.

CHAPTER TWENTY-THREE

LESSONS

"The music is not in the notes, but in the silence in between."[1]
Wolfgang Amadeus Mozart

WHAT'S the best decision you ever made?

Other than proposing to my wife and deciding to become a teacher, learning how to play guitar has been my best decision. It gives me the opportunity to learn about myself, validates the fact that I am on the right path, and provides me with a great deal of joy and personal fulfillment. Most importantly, especially for a retiree, guitar fills my life with purpose and meaning. It allows me, at least in my own mind, to remain relevant in the world.

The lessons I've learned from playing guitar mirror the lessons I've learned in life. First, hard work and persistence pays off. Don't give up. Second, failure breeds success. I have failed thousands of times while learning new songs, but the ratio of failure to success eventually turns. Third, if you put your heart into any endeavor, you will receive more than you give. Fourth, it's difficult to realize your potential in life if you don't try something new, no matter your age. Fifth, if you are going to do something, try to do it to the best of your ability. Life is too short to waste time. Sixth, it's worth repeating: In order to fully realize potential, it's important to exercise, get enough sleep, and maintain a healthy diet. Seventh, it's important to know who we are as individuals. It's been my observation that many people don't know who they really are. They match the energy of other individuals instead of being true to themselves. This describes me when I was a young man. However, the older I get, the more I don't care what people think.

Finally, it's important to keep moving forward in life. I'm reminded of the last scene from the last episode from the *West Wing* series. The former president has just left office after serving two terms. His wife asked him, "What are you thinking about?" He replied, "Tomorrow." Even though it's important to live in the moment, guitar helps me to keep moving forward in life. It gives me hope in these dire times and sets me free. It's a gift of the highest order.

People can tell me they bought a new car, or a new house, or took a trip to Europe, or this or that. That is wonderful, but *I have a secret weapon in my house.* Forget about taking a trip around the world, my guitar can take me to places where human beings have yet to set foot. It's a feeling that money can't buy and my own sweat equity produced. Something that is so mystical and ethereal that the voodoo child himself could not put it into words.

Speaking of sweat equity, several years ago a study found that 81% of the younger generation believed the most important goal in life was to get rich.[2] My guess is some of those adolescents wanted to be wealthy without putting in the work it takes to become financially independent. It's sad because one of the greatest pleasures in life is the personal fulfillment of hard work and a job well done.

Another study found that winning the lottery resulted in

three years of stress due to cognitive dissonance, a phenomenon where the brain is confused. The researchers found that the angst of winning the lottery was eliminated only when the winners believed their money was earned and they deserved it. [3] Now, what does this have to do with playing guitar? Well, one of the best things about guitar is that even though I have to work hard at it, the reward is mind-blowing. I could literally wake up in the middle of the night, pick up my guitar, and launch into a Bruce Springsteen/Green Day/Doobie Brothers/Neil Young/Led Zeppelin mashup. But I can only do that because of the time I put in. Even after playing for five years, there are moments when I still can't believe what I'm doing on the fretboard. It's the greatest reward I can imagine, and satisfaction of the highest order. I wish everyone could experience what it feels like.

In this day and age of fear and anxiety, people rely on music for many things, whether it's comfort, distraction, or entertainment. Individuals use music to share feelings, get in touch with themselves, or help them feel better when they're feeling down. Perhaps most importantly, music provides meaning to our lives by helping us to think about who we are and where we're going.

No one really knows, but my guess is billions of people listen to music every day. Which begs the question, is there anyone who does not like music? The answer is yes, 3-5% of healthy individuals do not experience pleasure when they listen to music, a condition known as specific musical anhedonia.[4] Consequently, it's possible that over 300 million people don't like music. I am curious if these individuals share my distaste for background music. If so, how do they cope with music seemingly everywhere in the public domain?

Many individuals do not think about the benefits music provides, as it can be taken for granted. However, music plays many roles in our lives and we depend on it. Indeed, music is always there, the best friend you could ever have. Toward that end, music is similar to a family pet in that it is a member of the family. After all, where would you be without it? Imagine if music ceased to exist. What impact would that have on your life?

Love and music are the greatest gifts bestowed upon humanity. Truly, music seems to be the answer to many of life's problems. Music launches me into a time-warp vortex where I can touch the stars, find life in black holes, and live for eternity. It's like taking a tequila shot of energy from the center of the sun and then hitching a ride on a rocket ship to another galaxy.

It's just me, a piece of wood, and six strings.

CHAPTER TWENTY-FOUR

LIFETIME LIST OF 700 FAVORITE SONGS

HERE'S my life in songs, a list of my favorite songs at one time or another since I began listening to music in 1967. Interestingly, 700 songs is an average of approximately one a month over the course of 53 years. I'm sure I forgot some songs but this is the best I could do.

- Abba: Dancing Queen
- AC/DC: Highway to Hell
- AC/DC: You Shook Me All Night Long
- Ace: How Long
- Adam Lambert: Whataya Want from Me
- Adele: Hello
- Aerosmith: Sweet Emotion
- Aerosmith: Walk This Way
- A Great Big World: Younger
- A Great Big World: Say Something
- Alan Jackson: Remember When
- Alan Parsons Project: Voyager
- Alan Parsons Project: The Eagle Will Rise Again

- Alicia Keys: If I Ain't Got You
- Alicia Keys: Teenage Love Affair
- Alicia Keys: Empire State of Mind
- Amanda Marshall: Let It Rain
- America: Ventura Highway
- America: A Horse with No Name
- Andy Williams: Moon River
- Annie Lennox: Why
- April Wine: Say Hello
- Average White Band: Work to Do
- Avril Lavigne: I'm With You
- Bachman –Turner Overdrive: Let It Ride
- Bachman –Turner Overdrive: You Ain't Seen Nothing Yet
- Bad Company: Feel Like Makin' Love
- Badfinger: Day After Day
- Barbra Streisand: The Way We Were
- Barbra Streisand / Neil Diamond: You Don't Bring Me Flowers
- Barry Manilow: Mandy
- Barry White: Can't Get Enough of Your Love, Babe
- Beach Boys: God Only Knows
- Beach Boys: Wouldn't It Be Nice
- Beach Boys: Good Vibrations
- Beatles: Let It Be
- Beatles: Lucy in the Sky with Diamonds
- Beatles: With a Little Help from My Friends
- Beth Nielsen Chapman: Sand and Water
- Better Than Ezra: Desperately Wanting
- Better Than Ezra: At the Stars
- Better Than Ezra: A Lifetime
- Big & Rich: Baby When I Look at You
- Bill Withers: Ain't No Sunshine
- Billy Idol: Eyes Without A Face

- Billy Joel: Piano Man
- Billy Joel: She's Always a Woman to Me
- Billy Joel: Vienna
- Billy Ocean: Caribbean Queen
- Billy Ocean: Get Outta My Dreams Get Into My Car
- Billy Porter: Time
- Billy Preston: Outa Space
- B.J. Thomas: Raindrops Keep Falling on My Head
- Billy Thorpe: Children of the Sun
- Blackmill: Embrace
- Blake Shelton: God Gave Me You
- Blood, Sweat & Tears: Spinning Wheel
- Blue Oyster Cult: Don't Fear the Reaper
- Blue Swede: Hooked on a Feeling
- Bob Dylan: The Times They Are a-Changin'
- Bob Dylan: Knockin' on Heaven's Door
- Bob Dylan: Lay Lady Lay
- Bob Seger: Night Moves
- Bob Seger: We've Got Tonight
- Bon Jovi: Wanted Dead or Alive
- Bonnie Raitt: I Can't Make You Love Me
- Book Of Love: You Make Me Feel So Good
- Boston: More Than a Feeling
- Boz Skaggs: Lowdown
- Brad Paisley: Last Time for Everything
- Bread: If
- Bread: Make It with You
- Bread: Everything I Own
- Bread: Baby I'm-a Want You
- Brett Young: Mercy
- Bruce Springsteen: Born to Run
- Bruce Springsteen: My Hometown
- Bruce Springsteen: Secret Garden
- Bruce Springsteen: The Rising

- Bruce Springsteen: She's the One
- Bruce Springsteen: Land of Hope and Dreams
- Bruce Springsteen: Dancing in the Dark
- Bruce Springsteen: One Step Up
- Bruno Mars: 24K Magic
- Boney James: Blue
- Brother Bones: Sweet Georgia Brown
- Bruce Hornsby and the Range: Mandolin Rain
- Bruce Hornsby and the Range: The Way It Is
- Bryan Adams: Summer of 69
- Bryan Adams: Cuts Like a Knife
- Bryan Adams: When You Love Someone
- Bryan Adams: Somebody
- Buffalo Springfield: For What It's Worth
- B.W. Stevenson: My Maria
- Candy Dulfer: For the Love of You
- Candy Dulfer: Smooth
- Candy Dulfer: Allright
- Carol King: It's Too Late
- Camel: Wing and a Prayer
- Carly Rae Jepsen: Call Me Maybe
- Carly Simon: Anticipation
- Carly Simon: You're So Vain
- Carrie Underwood: Southbound
- Cat Stevens: Morning Has Broken
- Cat Stevens: The Wind
- Cat Stevens: Oh Very Young
- Celine Dion: My Heart Will Go On
- Cheryl Lynn: Got to Be Real
- Chicago: Just You and Me
- Chicago: Saturday in the Park
- Chicago: Feelin' Stronger Every Day
- Chilliwack: Fly at Night
- Chris Lane: Take Back Home Girl

- Chris Stapleton: Fire Away
- Christopher Cross: Sailing
- Clannad: Harry's Game
- Colbie Caillat: Realize
- Coldplay: Army of One
- Coldplay: Everglow
- Coldplay: Paradise
- Coldplay: Magic
- Coldplay: Fix You
- Coldplay: Clocks
- Cornelius Brothers and Sister Rose: Treat Her Like a Lady
- Cornelius Brothers and Sister Rose: Too Late to Turn Back Now
- Counting Crows: Round Here
- Counting Crows: Children in Bloom
- Counting Crows: Raining in Baltimore
- Creedence Clearwater Revival: Have You Ever Seen the Rain
- Creedence Clearwater Revival: Fortunate Son
- Creedence Clearwater Revival: Up Around the Bend
- Creedence Clearwater Revival: Down on the Corner
- Creedence Clearwater Revival: Who'll Stop the Rain
- Creedence Clearwater Revival: Born on the Bayou
- Crosby, Stills and Nash: Teach Your Children
- Crosby, Stills and Nash: Helplessly Hoping
- Crosby, Stills and Nash: Suite Judy Blue Eyes
- Crosby, Stills, Nash and Young: Carry On
- Curtis Mayfield: Superfly
- Cyndi Lauper: Time After Time
- Cyndi Lauper: True Colors
- Dave Mason: World in Changes
- Dave Mason: We Just Disagree
- David Bowie: Rebel Rebel

- David Bowie: Fame
- David Bowie/Queen: Under Pressure
- David Sanborn: Just for You
- Dead Can Dance: American Dreamer
- Deana Carter: Strawberry Wine
- Deep Blue Something: Breakfast at Tiffany's
- Deep Purple: Gettin' Tighter
- Def Leppard: Photograph
- Def Leppard: Pour Some Sugar on Me
- Diamond Rio: One More Day
- Diana Ross: Touch Me in the Morning
- Diana Ross: Ain't No Mountain High Enough
- Diana Ross: I'm Coming Out
- DJ Jazzy Jeff and the Fresh Prince: Summertime
- DJ Shadow: Ashes to Oceans
- Dionne Warwick: This Girl's in Love with You
- Dionne Warwick: I Say a Little Prayer
- Dionne Warwick: I'll Never Fall in Love Again
- Dionne Warwick: What the World Needs Now Is Love
- Dionne Warwick: Walk On By
- Dionne Warwick: Do You Know the Way to San Jose
- Dionne Warwick: Alfie
- Dionne Warwick: Make It Easy on Yourself
- Dobie Gray: Drift Away
- Don Henley: The Boys of Summer
- Donny Hathaway: A Song for You
- Eagles: I Can't Tell You Why
- Eagles: Already Gone
- Eagles: Take It Easy
- Earth, Wind and Fire: That's the Way of the World
- Earth, Wind and Fire: Devotion
- Eddie Money: Take Me Home Tonight
- Eddie Money: Two Tickets to Paradise
- Electric Light Orchestra: Fire on High

- Eli Young Band: Skin and Bones
- Elton John: Your Song
- Elton John: Someone Saved My Life Tonight
- Elton John: Candle in the Wind
- Elton John: Bennie and the Jets
- Elton John: Tiny Dancer
- Emerson, Lake and Palmer: From the Beginning
- Emotions: Best of My Love
- Enigma: Return to Innocence
- Ennio Morricone: Love Theme from *Cinema Paradiso*
- Enya: Caribbean Blue
- Enya: Shepherd Moons
- Enya: Storms in Africa
- Enya: Watermark
- Enya: On Your Shore
- Enya: River
- Enya: Building a Mystery
- Enya: Angel
- Enya: I Want Tomorrow
- Eric Burden: Spill the Wine
- Eric Church: Record Year
- Eric Church: Mr. Misunderstood
- Eric Church: Talladega
- Eric Church: Homeboy
- Eric Serra: The Big Blue Overture from *The Big Blue*
- Eva Cassidy: Fields of Gold
- Everything But The Girl: Driving
- Everything But The Girl: Rollercoaster
- Everything But The Girl: Two Star
- Everything But The Girl: Old Friends
- Everything But The Girl: Understanding
- Everything But The Girl: Downtown Train
- Everything But The Girl: British Summertime
- Everything But The Girl: One Place

- Everything But The Girl: 25th December
- Everything But The Girl: Boxing and Pop Music
- Everything But The Girl: No Difference
- Everything But The Girl: Take Me
- Everything But The Girl: My Baby Don't Love Me
- Everything But The Girl: Single
- Everything But The Girl: The Heart Remains a Child
- Faith Hill: When the Lights Go Down
- Fleetwood Mac: Landslide
- Fleetwood Mac: Gypsy
- Fleetwood Mac: Sara
- Fleetwood Mac: Silver Springs
- Flock of Seagulls: I Ran (So Far Away)
- Florence and the Machine: The End of Love
- Focus: Hocus Pocus
- Frank Sinatra: It Was a Very Good Year
- Free: All Right Now
- Fuel: Hemorrhage
- Gabriel Yard: The Lover
- Garth Brooks: I Hope You Dance
- Gary Clark: Pearl Cadillac
- Gary Wright: Dream Weaver
- Gary Wright: Love Is Alive
- General Public: Tenderness
- Genesis: Throwing It All Away
- Genesis: In Too Deep
- George Harrison: My Sweet Lord
- George Michael: Careless Whisper
- George Strait: Check Yes or No
- George Winston: Colors/Dance
- George Winston: Jesus, Jesus, Rest Your Head
- George Winston: The Venice Dreamer
- George Winston: Longing
- George Winston: Peace

- George Winston: Thanksgiving
- George Winston: Carol of the Bells
- George Winston: Living in the Country
- George Winston: Stars
- George Winston: Hummingbird
- George Winston: The Garden
- George Winston: Moon
- George Winston: Many Clocks
- George Winston: Variations on Canon
- Giraffage: Feels
- Glen Campbell: Wichita Lineman
- Glen Campbell: Galveston
- Goo Goo Dolls: Iris
- Gordon Lightfoot: Sundown
- Go West: Call Me
- Go West: Goodbye Girl
- Grand Funk Railroad: We're an American Band
- Grand Funk Railroad: I'm Your Captain/Closer to Home
- Green Day: Good Riddance
- Greg Kihn Band: Jeopardy
- Halsey: Graveyard
- Hamilton, Joe Frank and Reynolds: Don't Pull Your Love
- Haux: Caves
- Head East: Never Been Any Reason
- Heart: Alone
- Heart: What About Love
- Heart: Dreamboat Annie
- Heart: Magic Man
- Heart: Crazy on You
- Heather Nova: Widescreen
- Il Divo: Time to Say Goodbye
- Il Divo: Somewhere

- Illenium: With You
- Isaac Hayes: Theme from Shaft
- Imogen Heap: Hide and Seek
- Jackson Browne: Running on Empty
- Jackson Browne: That Girl Could Sing
- Jackson Browne: The Barricades of Heaven
- Jackson Browne: Doctor My Eyes
- Jackson Browne: Boulevard
- Jackson Browne: The Load Out
- James Blunt: You're Beautiful
- James Taylor: You've Got a Friend
- James Taylor: Sweet Baby James
- Jane's Addiction: Jane Says
- Jann Arden: I Would Die for You
- Jean Knight: Mr. Big Stuff
- Jesse Cook: Virtue
- Jewel: Good Day
- Jimi Hendrix: All Along the Watchtower
- Jimi Hendrix: Fire
- Jimmy Ray: Are You Jimmy Ray
- Jimmy Ray: Look Inside for Love
- Jim Rickman: Rocket to the Moon
- Jim Rickman: Angel Eyes
- Joan Baez: Diamonds and Rust
- John Cougar Mellencamp: Small Town
- John Cougar Mellencamp: Pink Houses
- John Cougar Mellencamp: Jack & Diane
- John Cougar Mellencamp: Dance Naked
- John Coltrane: Welcome
- John Coltrane: Soul Lies
- John Denver: Rocky Mountain High
- John Hiatt: Have a Little Faith in Me
- Johnny Nash: I Can See Clearly Now
- John Parr: St. Elmo's Fire

- John Waite: Every Time I Think of You
- John Waite: Change
- Joni Mitchell: Both Sides Now
- Joni Mitchell: Help Me
- Joni Mitchell: Big Yellow Taxi
- Joni Mitchell: River
- Joni Mitchell: Woodstock
- Josh Ritter: Homecoming
- Journey: Nickel and Dime
- Journey: Topaz
- Journey: In the Morning Day
- Journey: Of a Lifetime
- Journey: I Would Find You
- Journey: Open Arms
- Journey: Faithfully
- Julia Fordham: Porcelain
- Julia Fordham: Manhattan Skyline
- Kansas: Carry On Wayward Son
- Kate Bush: This Woman's Work
- Katy Perry: Wide Awake
- Katy Perry: Teenage Dream
- Katy Perry: Daisies
- Katrina and the Waves: Walking on Sunshine
- KC and the Sunshine Band: Please Don't Go
- Kelsea Ballerini: Homecoming Queen
- Keith Urban: Raise 'Em Up
- Keith Urban: We Were
- Keith Urban: Stupid Boy
- Kenny Chesney: California
- Kenny Chesney: There Goes My Life
- Kenny Chesney: Setting the World on Fire
- Kenny Chesney: Don't Blink
- Kevin Cadogan: Further Than the Stars
- Kevin Cadogan: Surfacing Submarine

- King Harvest: Dancing in the Moonlight
- Lady Antebellum: What If I Never Get Over You
- Lady Gaga and Bradley Cooper: Shallow
- LANCO: Greatest Love Story
- LeAnn Rimes: Probably Wouldn't Be This Way
- Led Zeppelin: Babe I'm Gonna Leave You
- Led Zeppelin: What Is and What Should Never Be
- Led Zeppelin: The Rain Song
- Led Zeppelin: Over the Hills and Far Away
- Led Zeppelin: Tangerine
- Led Zeppelin: Black Dog
- Led Zeppelin: Kashmir
- Lee Michaels: Do You Know What I Mean
- Lemongrass: Feel Good
- Len: Steal My Sunshine
- LeVert: Casanova
- LFO: Girl on TV
- Lifehouse: Whatever It Takes
- Linda Ronstadt/Aaron Neville: Don't Know Much
- Lindsey Buckingham: Trouble
- Linkin Park: In the End
- Lisa Stansfield: All Around the World
- Lisa Stansfield: The Real Thing
- Little Big Town: Better Man
- Little Big Town: Girl Crush
- Looking Glass: Brandy
- Lou Gramm: Midnight Blue
- Louis Armstrong: What a Wonderful World
- Lou Reed: Sweet Jane
- Lou Reed: Heroin
- Love Unlimited Orchestra: Walkin' in the Rain with the One I Love
- Luciano Pavarotti: Nessun dorma (from *Turandot*)
- Lukas Nelson and Promise of the Real: Pali Gap/Hey

Baby (New Rising Sun)
- Luke Bryan: Play It Again
- Lulu: To Sir with Love
- Luther Vandross: Superstar
- Luther Vandross: A House Is Not a Home
- Madonna: Borderline
- Madonna: Lucky Star
- Madonna: Holiday
- Madonna: Don't Cry for Me Argentina
- Manfred Mann's Earth Band: Blinded by the Light
- Marc Antoine: Sunland
- Maren Morris: The Middle
- Mark Cohn: Walking in Memphis
- Martina McBride: I'm Gonna Love You Through It
- Martina McBride: In My Daughter's Eyes
- Marvin Gaye: What's Going On
- Marvin Gaye: Mercy Mercy Me
- Marvin Gaye: Let's Get It On
- Marvin Gaye: Sexual Healing
- MGMT: Time to Pretend
- Michael Franti and Spearhead: Oh My God
- Michael Jackson: Man in the Mirror
- Michael Jackson: Don't Stop 'til You Get Enough
- Michael Jackson: Pretty Young Thing
- Michael Nyman: Theme from *The Piano*
- Minnie Riperton: Lovin' You
- Michelle Branch: You Set Me Free
- Mike Monday: When the Rain Falls
- Miles Davis: It Never Entered My Mind
- Moby: God Moving over the Face of the Waters
- Moby: Porcelain
- Montrose: We're Going Home
- Montrose: Bad Motor Scooter
- Montrose: Make It Last

- Montrose: Space Station #5
- Montrose: Rock Candy
- Montrose: Rock the Nation
- Mozella: Amazed
- Mazzy Star: Fade Into You
- Nancy Sinatra: These Boots Are Made for Walkin'
- Naughty by Nature: O.P.P.
- Naughty by Nature: Feel Me Flow
- Nazareth: Hair of the Dog
- Neil Diamond: Cherry Cherry
- Neil Diamond: Sweet Caroline
- Neil Young: Old Man
- Neil Young: After the Gold Rush
- Neil Young: Hey Hey My My
- Nektar: Remember the Future
- Nelly Furtado: Say It Right
- Neon Trees: Sleeping with a Friend
- Nick Lachey: What's Left of Me
- Night Ranger: Sister Christian
- Nik Kershaw: Wouldn't It Be Good
- Nitty Gritty Dirt Band: Mr. Bojangles
- Old Dominion: Written in the Sand
- Old Dominion: One Man Band
- Old Dominion: Song for Another Time
- Oleta Adams: Get Here
- Oliver Tank: The Last Time
- Oliver Tank: I Love You
- Oliver Tank: Up All Night
- One Republic: Apologize
- Ozark Mountain Daredevils: Jackie Blue
- Patti Smith Group: Because the Night
- Paul Mauriat: Love Is Blue
- Paul McCartney: Maybe I'm Amazed
- Paul McCartney and Wings: Band on the Run

- Peter Gabriel: In Your Eyes
- Peter Gabriel: Red Rain
- Peter Gabriel: The Book of Love
- Peter White: Promenade
- Pete Townsend: Let My Love Open the Door
- Pet Shop Boys: West End Girls
- Petula Clark: Downtown
- Phantom of the Opera: Music of the Night
- Phil Collins: In the Air Tonight
- Phil Collins: The Roof Is Leaking
- Phil Collins: If Leaving Me Is Easy
- Phil Collins: You Know What I Mean
- Phil Collins: Hand in Hand
- Phoenix: 1901
- Pilot: Magic
- Pink: What About Us
- Pink Floyd: Have a Cigar
- Pink Floyd: Wish You Were Here
- Pink Floyd: Comfortably Numb
- Player: Baby Come Back
- P.M. Dawn: Set Adrift on Memory Bliss
- Poco: Sittin' on a Fence
- Poison: Every Rose Has Its Thorn
- Poison: Nothin' but a Good Time
- Poison: Something to Believe In
- Porcupine Tree: Voyage 34
- Porcupine Tree: Trains
- Pretenders: Birds of Paradise
- Pretenders: Waste Not Want Not
- Pretenders: Back on the Chain Gang
- Pretenders: The Wait
- Prince: Purple Rain
- Pure Prairie League: Amie
- Raspberries: Go All the Way

- Rick James: Super Freak
- Rick Springfield: Jessie's Girl
- Righteous Brothers: Unchained Melody
- Rihanna (Ft. Drake): Work
- Ringo Starr: It Don't Come Easy
- Rod Stewart: Maggie May
- Roger Williams: Born Free
- Rose Royce: Love Don't Live Here Anymore
- Roxette: Listen to Your Heart
- Roxy Music: Avalon
- Rufus and Chaka Khan: Ain't Nobody
- Rush: Xanadu
- Sam Cooke: Another Saturday Night
- Sammy Hagar: Young Girl Blues
- Sammy Hagar: Silver Lights
- San Holo: Light
- Santana: Europa
- Santana: Aqua Marine
- Santana (ft. Michelle Branch): The Game of Love
- Sara Bareilles: Gravity
- Sarah McLachlan: Angel
- Sarah McLachlan: Building a Mystery
- Sarah McLachlan: I Will Remember You
- Seasons of Love: (from *Rent*) The Sound and Musical Orchestra
- Shallou: Truth
- Shelby Lynne: Killin' Kind
- Shelby Lynne: Dreamsome
- Shenandoah: I Want to Be Loved Like That
- Shifty: Slide Along Side
- Simon and Garfunkel: Bridge Over Troubled Water
- Simon and Garfunkel: Scarborough Fair
- Simon and Garfunkel: Cecilia
- Simon and Garfunkel: Mrs. Robinson

- Simon and Garfunkel: The Sound of Silence
- Slushii: Sapient Dream
- Sly & the Family Stone: Dance to the Music
- Sly & the Family Stone: Thank You (Falettinme Be Mice Elf Agin)
- Sophie B. Hawkins: As I Lay Me Down
- Spandau Ballet: True
- Spyro Gyra: Joyride
- Starland Vocal Band: Afternoon Delight
- Steely Dan: Dirty Work
- Steely Dan: Rikki Don't Lose That Number
- Steely Dan: Reelin' in the Years
- Steppenwolf: Born to Be Wild
- Steve Winwood: Higher Love
- Stevie Wonder: My Cherie Amour
- Stevie Wonder: Isn't She Lovely
- St. Lucia: Love Somebody
- Stories: Brother Louie
- Styx: Come Sail Away
- Styx: Lady
- Sugarland: Every Girl Like Me
- Sugarloaf: Green-Eyed Lady
- Supertramp: Just Another Nervous Wreck
- Supertramp: Even in the Quietest Moments
- Supertramp: Downstream
- Supertramp: From Now On
- Supertramp: Fool's Overture
- Supertramp: Give a Little Bit
- Sweet: Love Is Like Oxygen
- Swing Out Sister: Twilight World
- Talking Heads: And She Was
- Talking Heads: Once in a Lifetime
- Tears For Fears: Everybody Wants to Rule the World
- 10cc: I'm Not in Love

- Ten Years After: I'd Love to Change the World
- The Association: Windy
- The Babys: Over and Over
- The Babys: I Believe in Love
- The Babys: Isn't It Time
- The Babys: Dying Man
- The Band Perry: When I Die Young
- The Box Tops: The Letter
- The Byrds: Mr. Tambourine Man
- The Carpenters: Close to You
- The Carpenters: Rainy Days and Mondays
- The Carpenters: We've Only Just Begun
- The Cars: Drive
- The Cars: My Best Friend's Girl
- The Cars: You're All I've Got Tonight
- The Cars: Just What I Needed
- The Cars: Bye-Bye Love
- The Church: Under the Milky Way
- The Commodores: Easy
- The Commodores: Sweet Love
- The Commodores: Sail On
- The Commodores: Three Times a Lady
- The Corrs: When the Stars Go Blue
- The Cranberries: Linger
- The Cranberries: Why
- The Cure: Friday I'm in Love
- The Cure: Lullaby
- The Cure: Love Song
- The Doobie Brothers: Neil's Fandango
- The Doobie Brothers: Sweet Maxine
- The Doobie Brothers: Road Angel
- The Doobie Brothers: Jesus Is Just Alright
- The Doobie Brothers: China Grove
- The Doobie Brothers: Long Train Runnin'

- The Doobie Brothers: Without You
- The Doobie Brothers: Natural Thing
- The Doobie Brothers: The Captain and Me
- The Doobie Brothers: Clear as the Driven Snow
- The Doobie Brothers: Ukiah
- The Doors: Break on Through (To the Other Side)
- The Dramatics: Whatcha See Is Whatcha Get
- The Fifth Dimension: Wedding Bell Blues
- The Fifth Dimension: One Less Bell to Answer
- The Fifth Dimension: Never My Love
- The Grass Roots: Temptation Eyes
- The Guess Who: These Eyes
- The Guess Who: No Sugar Tonight
- The Guess Who: No Time
- The Guess Who: Undun
- The Hollies: Long Cool Woman
- The Human League: Don't You Want Me
- The Human League: Human
- The Isley Brothers: Who's That Lady
- The Jackson 5: I'll Be There
- The Jackson 5: I Want You Back
- The Jackson 5: ABC
- The J. Geils Band: Love Stinks
- The Kinks: Lola
- The Knack: My Sharona
- The Mamas and Papas: California Dreamin'
- The Monkeys: I'm a Believer
- The Naked and Famous: Youngblood
- The Police: Wrapped Around Your Finger
- The Police: Walking on the Moon
- The Police: Voices Inside My Head
- The Police: Message in a Bottle
- The Police: Roxanne
- The Proclaimers: I Would Walk 500 Miles

- The Rolling Stones: Thru and Thru
- The Rolling Stones: Wild Horses
- The Rolling Stones: Brown Sugar
- The Rolling Stones: Waiting on a Friend
- The Rolling Stones: Sympathy for the Devil
- The Romantics: What I Like About You
- The Romantics: Talking in Your Sleep
- The Script: Breakeven
- The Spinners: I'll Be Around
- The Style Council: My Ever-Changing Moods
- The Stylistics: You Make Me Feel Brand New
- The Supremes: You Can't Hurry Love
- The Tubes: She's a Beauty
- The Turtles: Happy Together
- The Verve: Bitter Sweet Symphony
- The Who: Eminence Front
- The Who: Baba O'Riley
- The Who: Pinball Wizard
- The Zombies: Time of the Season
- Third Eye Blind: Losing a Whole Year
- Third Eye Blind: How's It Going to Be
- Third Eye Blind: Never Let You Go
- Third Eye Blind: Deep Inside of You
- Third Eye Blind: Crystal Baller
- Third Eye Blind: Blinded
- Third Eye Blind: The Red Summer Sun
- Third Eye Blind: Wounded
- Third Eye Blind: Don't Give In
- Third Eye Blind: Jumper
- 38 Special: Hold on Loosely
- Thompson Square: Are You Gonna Kiss Me or Not
- Three Dog Night: One
- Three Dog Night: Chest Fever
- Three Dog Night: Eli's Coming

- Three Dog Night: Joy to the World
- Three Dog Night: An Old Fashioned Love Song
- Tim McGraw: Red Rag Top
- Tim McGraw: Humble and Kind
- Todd Rundgren: Hello It's Me
- Todd Rundgren: Can We Still Be Friends
- Tommie Roe: Dizzy
- Tommy Bolin: People People
- Tommy Bolin: Wild Dogs
- Tommy Bolin: Post Toastee
- Tommy James and the Shondells: Crimson and Clover
- Tommy James and the Shondells: Crystal Blue Persuasion
- Tom Petty: Free Fallin'
- Tom Petty and the Heartbreakers: Learning to Fly
- Tom Petty and the Heartbreakers: Breakdown
- Tom Petty and the Heartbreakers: Don't Come Around Here No More
- Tom Petty and the Heartbreakers: The Wild One, Forever
- Tom Petty and the Heartbreakers: American Girl
- Tone-Loc: Funky Cold Medina
- Tori Amos: Tear in Your Hand
- Toto: Rosanna
- Tower of Power: So Very Hard to Go
- Tracy Chapman: Fast Car
- Tracy Chapman: Talkin' Bout a Revolution
- Tracy Thorne: Easy
- Traffic: The Low Spark of High Heeled Boys
- Train: Hey Soul Sister
- Trisha Yearwood: Georgia Rain
- Uriah Heap: The Wizard
- U2: One
- U2: With or Without You

- U2: Beautiful Day
- Van: Show Me Love
- Vancouver Sleep Clinic: Flaws
- Vangelis: Theme from *Chariots of Fire*
- Van Morrison: These Are the Days
- Van Morrison: Into the Mystic
- Van Morrison: I'll Be Your Lover Too
- Vonda Shepard: Maryland
- Washed Out: Feel It All Around
- War: The World Is a Ghetto
- War: The Cisco Kid
- Warren Zevon: Lawyers, Guns and Money
- Whitesnake: There I Go Again
- Whitney Houston: I Will Always Love You
- Willie Nelson: Always on My Mind
- X Ambassadors: Unsteady
- YES: Roundabout
- YES: Yours Is No Disgrace
- YES: Long Distance Runaround
- Zac Brown Band: Highway 20 Ride

REFERENCES

Introduction

1. Crowe, C., Bryce, I. (Producers), & Crowe, C. (Director). (2000). *Almost Famous.* [Motion Picture]. United States: Columbia Pictures DreamWorks Pictures Vinyl Films.

Chapter 1

1. Jagger, M., Richards, K., Wood, R., Watts, C. (2003). *According to the Rolling Stones*. George Weidenfeld & Nicholson.

2. Nelson, W., Pipkin, T. (2006). *The Tao of Willie: A Guide to the Happiness in Your Heart*. Gotham Books.

3. Paisley, B. (2011). *Diary of a Player: How My Musical Heroes Made a Guitar Man Out Of Me*. Howard Books.

Chapter 2

1. Plato. (1943). *Plato's The Republic*. New York Books, Inc.

2. Daltrey, R. (2018). *Thanks a Lot Mr. Kibblewhite: My Story/Roger Daltrey*. St Martin's Griffin. New York.

3. Zatorre R. J., Peretz I. (2001). The *Biological Foundations of Music.* New York, NY: New York Academy of Sciences

4. The Knack – Awards."*AllMusic*. Archived from *the original* on May 26, 2015. *Retrieved June 30, 2019*.

5. Crowe, C., Bryce, I. (Producers), & Crowe, C. (Director). (2000). *Almost Famous*. [Motion Picture]. United States: Columbia Pictures DreamWorks Pictures Vinyl Films.

6. University College London. (2016, June 2). Declining dopamine may explain why older people take fewer risks. *ScienceDaily*. Retrieved May 12, 2020 from www.sciencedaily.com/releases/2016/06/160602132424.htm

7. Mcdonald, G., (2020, May 13). *Every Noise at Once*. Retrieved from Http://everynoise.com/engenremap.html

Chapter 3

1. Longfellow, H.L. (1835). *Outre-Mer: A Pilgrimage Beyond the Sea*.

2. bEarishpArrot. (2016, April 8). *Amazing guitarist playing only with his feet in Balboa Park, San Diego* [Video]. YouTube. Retrieved from https://youtu.be/8HwRRsfD3WA

3. VEVOVish. (2013, Feb. 5). *Green Day - Good Riddance (Time of Your Life) (LIVE IN JAPAN) HD*. {Video]. YouTube. Retrieved from https://www.youtube.com/watch?v=6KOPxFznbFs

Chapter 4

1. Bonaparte, N. (2020, May 14). *goodreads*. Retrieved from https://www.goodreads.com/quotes/search?utf8=%E2%9C%93&q=Music+is+what+tells+us+that+the+human+race+is+greater+than+we+realize&commit=Search

2. Kansas. (2015, Jan. 28). *We Knew It Was Going to Be a Hit*. [Video]. YouTube. Retrieved fromhttps://www.youtube.com/watch?v=OcjGqrNamP4

3. Hagar, S., Selvin, J. (2011). *RED: My Uncensored Life in Rock*. HarperCollins Publishers, Inc.

4. Bachman, R. (2011). *Vinyl Tap Stories*. Penguin Group.

Chapter 5

1. Marley, B. (2020, May 14). *goodreads*. Retrieved from https://www.goodreads.com/quotes/search?utf8=%E2%9C%93&q=One+good+thing+about+music%2C+when+it+hits+you%2C+you+feel+no+pain&commit=Search

2. Hamlin, J., Morris, K., (Producers). (2017, June 11). *Bruno Mars on his artistry: "I'm working hard for this."* [Television broadcast]. United States. CBS.

Chapter 6

1. Goethe, J.W. (2020). May 14. *goodreads*. Retrieved from https://www.goodreads.com/quotes/search?utf8=&q=Everything+is+hard+before+it+is+easy&commit=Search

2. Gladwell, M. (2008). *The Outliers*. Little, Brown and Company

Chapter 7

1. Kalantri, A. (2020, May 14). *goodreads*. Retrieved from https://www.goodreads.com/quotes/search?utf8=%E2%9C%93&q=Music+is+the+fastest+motivator+in+the+world&commit=Search

2. iVideosongs FREE Online Music Lessons. (2018, Feb 27). *How to Play Tom Sawyer by RUSH on Guitar*. [Video]. YouTube. Retrieved from https://www.youtube.com/watch?v=4OtV_2A6fSo

3. SGRox - playguitarsolos. (2017, July 4). *Guitar Solo close-up view - Alvin Lee - I'd Love To Change The World.* {Video]. YouTube. Retrieved from https://www.youtube.com/watch?v=3vgUj8n8e3U

4. Clydeman. (2006, September 18). *Johnny A - Witchita Lineman.* [Video]. YouTube. Retrieved from https://www.youtube.com/watch?v=fL3mvkZ6mVk

5. Rick Beato. (2019, July 8). *Top 20 acoustic guitar intros of all*

time. {Video]. YouTube. Retrieved fromhttps://www.youtube.com/watch?v=9UNuqYFP-pM

6. #mjmonday. (2017, Nov. 27). *Everybody Wants To Rule The World - Tears For Fears Cover*. {Video]. YouTube. Retrieved from https://www.youtube.com/watch?v=UnNGfeosScA

7. Gabriella9797. (2015, May 24). *(Aerosmith) Dream On - Gabriella Quevedo*. {Video]. YouTube. Retrieved from https://www.youtube.com/watch?v=s6XkM9ri9io

8. The Independent. (2017, Feb. 21). *Bruce Springsteen brings young fan up onstage to perform 'Growin' Up' with him*. {Video]. YouTube. Retrieved from https://www.youtube.com/watch?v=VVzi8tM2Qlw

Chapter 8

1. Sondheim, S. (2020, May 14). *goodreads*. Retrieved from https://www.goodreads.com/quotes/search?utf8=%E2%9C%93&q=If+I+cannot+fly%2C+let+me+sing&commit=Search

2. Daltrey, R. (2018). *Thanks a Lot Mr. Kibblewhite: My Story/Roger Daltrey*. St. Martin's Griffin. New York.

3. Fancourt D., Ockelford A., Belai A. The psychoneuroimmunological effects of music: A systematic review and a new model. Brain Behav Immun. 2014;36:15–26. doi: 10.1016/j.bbi.2013.10.014.

4. Vickhoff, B., Malmgren, H., Åströmm, R., Nyberg, G., Ekström, S., Engwall, M., Snygg, J., Nilssonn, M., and Jörnsten, R. (2013, July 9). *Music structure determines heart rate variability of singers*. Front. Psychol. https://doi.org/10.3389/fpsyg.2013.00334 Retrieved from https://www.frontiersin.org/articles/10.3389/fpsyg.2013.00334/full

Chapter 9

1. Manson, M. (2020, May 14). *goodreads*. Retrieved from https://www.goodreads.com/quotes/search?utf8=%E2%9C%

93&q=Music+is+the+strongest+form+of+magic&commit=Search

Chapter 10

1. Einstein, A. (2020, May 14). *goodreads*. Retrieved from https://www.goodreads.com/quotes/search?utf8=%E2%9C%93&q=I+see+my+life+in+terms+of+music&commit=Search

2. Shutup & Play - Guitar Tutorials. (2014, Oct. 25). *how to play "Over the Hills and Far Away" on guitar by "Led Zeppelin" - acoustic guitar lesson*. {Video]. YouTube. Retrieved from https://www.youtube.com/watch?v=-JvESMqWX0s

3. PrestonSteveWMMR. (2014, May 22). *Better Than Ezra - Desperately Wanting - Preston & Steve's Daily Rush.* {Video]. YouTube. Retrieved from https://www.youtube.com/watch?v=rvSYsIJgvdU

4. Zanes, W. (2015). *Petty: The Biography*. Henry Holt and Company. New York.

5. Megan Simon. (2010, Nov. 4). *Let My Love Open the Door (Cover)* {Video]. YouTube. Retrieved from https://www.youtube.com/watch?v=qojM3_x7rxw

6. John, E. (2019). *ME: Elton John*. Henry Holt.

7. Bachman, R. (2011). *Vinyl Tap Stories*. Penguin Group.

8. Morris, A. (2016, July 28). *Inside Halsey's Troubled Past, Chaotic Present. Rolling Stone.* Retrieved from -chaotic-present-97968/" https://www.rollingstone.com/music/music-features/inside-halseys-troubled-past-chaotic-present-97968/

Chapter 11

1. Roosevelt, T. (2020, May 14). *goodreads*. Retrieved from https://www.goodreads.com/quotes/search?utf8=%E2%9C%93&q=Do+what+you+can%2C+with+what+you+have%2C+where+you+are&commit=Search

2. Hippocrates. (2020, May 14). *goodreads*. Retrieved from

(https://www.goodreads.com/quotes/search?utf8=%E2%9C%93&q=hippocrates&commit=Search

3. Perlmutter, D. (2013). *Grain Brain*. Little, Brown Spark.

4. Heffron, T.M. (2013, Aug 01). *Sleep and Caffeine*. Retrieved from http://sleepeducation.org/news/2013/08/01/sleep-and-caffeine

5. Young, O., Young, S.R. (2002, April 23). *The pH Miracle: Balance Your Diet, Reclaim Your Health*. Grand Central Life & Style

6. Webmd. Caffiene Side Effects & Safety. Retrieved from https://www.webmd.com/vitamins/ai/ingredientmono-979/caffeine

7. Hayes J.A., Cox C. (2000). Immediate effects of a five-minute foot massage on patients in critical care. Complement Ther Nurs Midwifery. 2000;6:9–13.

8. Chen Y. F., Huang X. Y., Chien C. H., Cheng J. F. (2016). The effectiveness of diaphragmatic breathing relaxation training for reducing anxiety. *Perspect. Psychiatr. Care* 10.1111/ppc.12184 [Epub ahead of print].

Chapter 12

1. Nietzsche, F. (1997, June 1). *Twilight of the Idols*. Hackett Publishing Company, Inc.

2. Billboard Year-End Hot 100 singles of 1971. (1971, Dec. 25). Retrieved from https://en.wikipedia.org/wiki/Billboard_Year-End_Hot_100_singles_of_1971

3. The Ethan Hein Blog. (2010, Jan. 26). *Imogen Heap and artificial harmon*. Retrieved from https://www.ethanhein.com/wp/2010/imogen-heap/

Chapter 13

1. Plato. (2020, May 14). *goodreads*. Retrieved from https://www.goodreads.com/quotes/search?utf8=%E2%9C%93&q=I+would+teach+children+music%2C+physics%2C+and+philosophy%3B+but+most+importantly+music%2C+for+the+

patterns+in+music+and+all+the+arts+are+the+keys+to+learning&commit=Search

2. Bolin, T. (1975). *Teaser*. Retrieved from https://en.wikipedia.org/wiki/Teaser_(Tommy_Bolin_album)

3. Runtag, H. (2018, March 28). *Led Zeppelin's 'Houses of the Holy': 10 Things You Didn't Know.* Rolling Stone. Retrieved from https://www.rollingstone.com/music/music-features/led-zeppelins-houses-of-the-holy-10-things-you-didnt-know-204694/

4. Aledort, A. (2019, May 28). *How to Utilize Unusual Alternate Tunings Like Jimmy Page. Guitar World.* Retrieved from https://www.guitarworld.com/lessons/deep-how-utilize-unusual-alternate-tunings-style-led-zeppelin-s-jimmy-page

5. Paris, N. (2007, Sept, 13). *20 million Led Zeppelin fans rush for tickets.* The Telegraph. Retrieved from https://www.telegraph.co.uk/news/uknews/1562990/20-million-Led-Zeppelin-fans-rush-for-tickets.html

6. HBO. (Aug 13, 2018). *Christian Kirksey's Drumming Roots' Ep. 1 Clip | Hard Knocks: Training Camp w/ the Cleveland Brown.* {Video]. YouTube. *Retrieved from* https://www.youtube.com/watch?v=5jzVH-IMWtw

Chapter 14

1. James, O. (2020, May 14). *goodreads*. Retrieved from https://www.goodreads.com/quotes/search?utf8=%E2%9C%93&q=Music+is+my+higher+power&commit=Search

2. smyletuneage. (2012, Dec. 28). *HEART - STAIRWAY TO HEAVEN in HD - The Kennedy Center Honors LED ZEPPELIN, 2012.* {Video]. YouTube. Retrieved from https://www.youtube.com/watch?v=8e2fJfiddx4

Chapter 15

1. Springsteen, B. (2020, May 14). *goodreads*. Retrieved from https://www.goodreads.com/quotes/search?utf8=%

E2%9C%93&q=The+best+music...+is+essentially+there+to+provide+you+something+to+face+the+world+with&commit=Search

2. Crowe, C., Bryce, I. (Producers), & Crowe, C. (Director). (2000). *Almost Famous.* [Motion Picture]. United States: Columbia Pictures DreamWorks Pictures Vinyl Films.

3. Wikipedia. (2020, May 14). *List of awards and nominations received by Bruce Springsteen.* Retrieved from https://en.wikipedia.org/wiki/List_of_awards_and_nominations_received_by_Bruce_Springsteen

4. Springsteen, B. (2016). *Born to Run*. Simon and Schuster.

5. Barclay, J., Chadha, G., Daniel, J. (Producers). Chadha, G. (Director). (2019). *Blinded by the Light.* [Motion Picture]. Warner Bros.

6. Cooper, A., Zimmerman, K., Zimmerman, K. (2007). *Alice Cooper: Golf Monster: A Rock 'n Roller's 12 Steps to Becoming a Golf Addict.* Crown Publishers.

7. Crandall, Bill. (2014). "10 musicians who saw the Beatles standing there" Archived February 7, 2014, at the Wayback Machine, CBS News, February 6, 2014.

8. Daltrey, R. 2018. *Thanks a Lot Mr. Kibblewhite: My Story/Roger Daltrey*. St Martin's Griffin. New York.

9. Hendrix, L., Mitchell, A. (2012). *Jimi Hendrix: A Brother's Story*. St. Martin's Press.

10. Black 1999, pp. 16–18: Hendrix playing along with "Hound Dog" (secondary source); Hendrix 1999, p. 100: Hendrix playing along with Presley's version of "Hound Dog" (primary source); Hendrix & Mitchell 2012, p. 59: Hendrix playing along with Presley songs (primary source).

11. Heatley, M. (2009). *Jimi Hendrix Gear: The Guitars, Amps & Effects that Revolutionized Rock 'n' Roll.* Voyageur Press.

12. Salewicz, C. (2018). *Jimmy Page: The Definitive Biography.* London: HarperCollins.

13. Perry, J. (2014). *Rocks : My Life in and Out of Aerosmith.* Simon & Schuster, Inc.

14. Hagar, S., Selvin, J. (2011). *RED: My Uncensored Life in Rock.* HarperCollins Publishers, Inc.

15. Paisley, B. (2011). *Diary of a Player: How My Musical Heroes Made a Guitar Man Out Of Me.* Howard Books.

16. Thamel, P. (2004, Feb. 17). *BASKETBALL; In the Name Of His Father.* New York Times. Retrieved from https://www.nytimes.com/2004/02/17/sports/basketball-in-the-name-of-his-father.html

Chapter 16

1. Beethoven, L.V. (2020, May 15). *goodreads.* Retrieved from https://www.goodreads.com/quotes/search?utf8=%E2%9C%93&q=beethoven&commit=Search

2. Hagen, J. 2017. *Sticky Fingers: The Life and Times of Jann Wenner and Rolling Stone Magazine.* Alfred A. Knopf.

Chapter 17

1. Pollack, J. (2020, May 15). *goodreads.* Retrieved from https://www.goodreads.com/quotes/search?utf8=%E2%9C%93&q=Love+is+friendship+set+to+music&commit=Search

2. Crowe, C., Bryce, I. (Producers), & Crowe, C. (Director). (2000). *Almost Famous.* [Motion Picture]. United States: Columbia Pictures DreamWorks Pictures Vinyl Films.

3. Guinness World Records. (2012). Best-selling single." Archived from the original on 13 January 2018. Retrieved 11 January 2018.

4. Harris, Craig. "Ray Dorset – Artist Biography". AllMusic. Archived from the original on 27 January 2019. Retrieved 20 January 2019.

5. The Guardian. (2006, July 29). The essential summer mix". Archived from the original on 24 July 2015. Retrieved 10 February 2019.

6. Nightingale, Laura (7 October 2015). "Mungo Jerry celebrates 45 years of In the Summertime at Camberley Theatre". Get Surrey. Archived from the original on 27 January 2019. Retrieved 10 February 2019.

7. Murrells, J. (1978). *The Book of Golden Discs* (2nd, illustrated ed.). Barrie & Jenkins.

8. "Bill Haley Biography." Rock and Roll Hall of Fame. Archived from the original on 22 May 2010. Retrieved 13 November 2010.

9. ultimate-guitar.com (2020, May 15). *Top Tabs all-time*. Retrieved from https://www.ultimate-guitar.com/

10. TopMusicMafia. (2020, May 3). *Top 100 Most Viewed Songs Of All Time (May 2020)*. Retrieved from https://www.youtube.com/watch?v=YtvaNHxlCTw

11. Royalty Exchange. Three Things the Top 10 Royalty Earning Songs of All-Time Have in Common. https://www.royaltyexchange.com/blog/three-things-the-top-10-royalty-earning-songs-of-all-time-have-in-common

12. Trust, G. (May 9, 2014). *"Imagine Dragons' 'Radioactive' Ends Record Billboard Hot 100 Run"*. Billboard. Nielsen Business Media, Inc. *Archived* from the original on May 11, 2014. *Retrieved May 9, 2014.*

13. Rolling Stone. (2011, April 7). *500 Greatest Songs of All Time* Retrieved from https://www.rollingstone.com/music/music-lists/500-greatest-songs-of-all-time-151127/

14. Mullin, J. (2016, Feb. 10). Ars TECHNICA. *"Happy Birthday" is public domain, former owner Warner/Chapell to pay $14M.* Retrieved from https://arstechnica.com/tech-policy/2016/02/happy-birthday-is-public-domain-former-owner-warnerchapell-to-pay-14m/

Chapter 18

1. Hart, C. (2020, May 15). *goodreads*. Retrieved from https://www.goodreads.com/quotes/search?utf8=%E2%9C%93&q=

Softly%2C+deftly%2C+music+shall+caress+you.+Hear+it%2C+feel+it%2C+secretly+possess+you&commit=Search

Chapter 19

1. Swift, T. (2020, May 15). *goodreads*. Retrieved from https://www.goodreads.com/quotes/search?utf8=%E2%9C%93&q=People+haven%27t+always+been+there+for+me+the+music+always+has&commit=Search

2. The-Art-of-Guitar. (2019, Nov. 6). *Taylor Swift Might Be a Better Guitarist Than You! (9 Reasons).* {Video]. YouTube. Retrieved from Https://www.youtube.com/watch?v=YF1tx9KyhPc

3. McIntyre, H. (2020, Feb. 11). *Taylor Swift Sold More Singles In The Past Decade Than Any Other Musician.* Forbes. Retrieved from https://www.forbes.com/sites/hughmcintyre/2020/02/11/taylor-swift-sold-more-singles-in-the-past-decade-than-any-other-musician/#798a46847c5d

4. Silman, A. (2014, Oct. 30). *Inside One of Taylor Swift's Secret Listening Sessions.* Cosmopolitan. Retrieved from https://www.cosmopolitan.com/entertainment/celebs/a32667/inside-taylor-swifts-secret-listening-session/

Chapter 20

1. Waits, T. (2020, May 15). *goodreads*. Retrieved from https://www.goodreads.com/quotes/search?utf8=%E2%9C%93&q=The+universe+is+making+music+all+the+time&commit=Search

2. CDC: Centers for Disease Control and Prevention. (2020, May 15). *What Noises Cause Hearing Loss?* Retrieved from https://www.cdc.gov/nceh/hearing_loss/what_noises_cause_hearing_loss.html

3. Clercq, C., Goedegebure, A., Jaddoe, V., et al . (2018, Aug). *Association Between Portable Music Player Use and Hearing Loss Among Children of School Age in the Netherlands.* JAMA Otolaryngol Head Neck Surg. 2018;144(8):668-675.

doi:10.1001/jamaoto.2018.0646. Retrieved from https://jamanetwork.com/journals/jamaotolaryngology/article-abstract/2684510

Chapter 21

1. Kerouac, J. (2020, May 15). *goodreads.* Retrieved from https://www.goodreads.com/quotes/search?utf8=%E2%9C%93&q=The+only+truth+is+music&commit=Search

2. Norman's Rare Guitars. (2018, Feb. 10). *Some of the Greatest Moments at Norman's Rare Guitars - Part 1.* {Video]. YouTube. Retrieved from https://www.youtube.com/watch?v=AI1RhFYwAc4&t=181s

3. Chemtob, D. (2016, Dec. 16). A Long, Strange Trip Through San Francisco's Rock 'N' Roll History. culture trip. Retrieved from https://theculturetrip.com/north-america/usa/california/articles/a-long-strange-trip-through-san-franciscos-rock-n-roll-history/

4. Zanes, W. (2015). *Petty: The Biography.* Henry Holt and Company. New York.

Chapter 22

1. Shakespeare, W. (1602). *Twelfth Night.* Retrieved from https://www.goodreads.com/quotes/search?utf8=%E2%9C%93&q=If+music+be+the+food+of+love%2C+play+on&commit=Search

2. Liikkanen L.A. (2008) Music in everymind: Commonality of involuntary musical imagery. *Proceedings of the 10th International Conference of Music Perception and Cognition.* Sapporo, Japan.

3. Jakubowski, K., Finkel, S., Stewart, L., & Müllensiefen, D. (2017). Dissecting an earworm: Melodic features and song popularity predict involuntary musical imagery. *Psychology of Aesthetics, Creativity, and the Arts.* http://dx.doi.org/10.1037/aca0000090

4. Cheung, V., Harrison, P., Meyer, L., Pearce, M., Haynes, J., Koelsch, S. Current Biology. Volume 29, ISSUE 23, P4084-4092.e4, December 02, DOI: https://doi.org/10.1016/j.cub.2019.09.067

5. Saul, H. (2014, Nov.1). *Independent.* Scientists discover Spice Girls' anthem Wannabe is the catchiest song of all time. Retrieved from https://www.independent.co.uk/arts-entertainment/music/scientists-discover-spice-girls-anthem-wannabe-is-the-catchiest-song-of-all-time-9833040.html?cmpid=facebook-post

6. Carly Rae Jepsen. (2012, March 1). *Carly Rae Jepsen - Call Me Maybe.* [Video]. YouTube. Retrieved from https://www.youtube.com/watch?v=fWNaR-rxAic

Chapter 23

1. Mozart. W.A. (2020, June 7). *goodreads.* Retrieved from Https://www.goodreads.com/quotes/49752-the-music-is-not-in-the-notes-but-in-the

2. Rosenberg, Simon and Leyden, Peter. 2007. The Fifty-Year Strategy. Mother Jones, November, December, 65.

3. University of Zürich. 2009. Delay and Deservingness after Winning the Lottery. Winner's Remorse. The Atlantic, April, 17.

4. Mas-Herrero E, Zatorre RJ, Rodriguez-Fornells A, Marco-Pallarés J. (2014). *Dissociation between musical and monetary reward responses in specific musical anhedonia.* Curr Biol 24(6):699–704.

ACKNOWLEDGMENTS

I'd like to thank Hannah Linder for a wonderful cover and a beautifully-designed book. You stuck by me and I couldn't have done it without you.

To Chey King, thank you for your input and ongoing support.

Thank you Vanessa Gonsalves, Kimberly Henderson, Savannah Pascucci-Luevano, Doug Flockhart, and Barbara Bernard for your input.

I'd also like to extend my appreciation to my instructors and the local music stores who helped me along the way.

Thank you Keith for 50 years of friendship and helping me become a better guitar player.

To Tiffany and Ken, thank you for putting up with the noise.

I'm also grateful to the guitarists who have inspired me during the last 50 years: Tom Johnston, Patrick Simmons, Nancy Wilson, Jimmy Page, Bruce Springsteen, Kevin Cadogan, Neal Schon, Tommy Bolin, and Ronnie Montrose.

Finally, I couldn't have written this book without the love and support from my wonderful wife. I love you so much.

ABOUT THE AUTHOR

Dan Flockhart is a retired elementary and middle school teacher and a former advisor for elementary education students in higher education. He is the author of the *Fantasy Sports and Mathematics Series,* social justice programs to help students acquire a love for mathematics, close the achievement gap, and break out of the poverty cycle.

Made in the USA
Monee, IL
06 May 2021

67966199R00146